Surveillance, Privacy, and the Law

Law, Meaning, and Violence

The scope of Law, Meaning, and Violence is defined by the wide-ranging scholarly debates signaled by each of the words in the title. Those debates have taken place among and between lawyers, anthropologists, political theorists, sociologists, and historians, as well as literary and cultural critics. This series is intended to recognize the importance of such ongoing conversations about law, meaning, and violence as well as to encourage and further them.

Series Editors:

Martha Minow, Harvard Law School
Michael Ryan, Northeastern University
Austin Sarat, Amherst College

Narrative, Violence, and the Law: The Essays of Robert Cover,
edited by Martha Minow, Michael Ryan, and Austin Sarat

Narrative, Authority, and Law, by Robin West

*The Possibility of Popular Justice: A Case Study of Community
Mediation in the United States,* edited by Sally Merry and
Neal Milner

Legal Modernism, by David Luban

*Surveillance, Privacy, and the Law: Employee Drug Testing and
the Politics of Social Control,* by John Gilliom

Surveillance, Privacy, and the Law

*Employee Drug Testing
and the Politics
of Social Control*

John Gilliom

Ann Arbor

THE UNIVERSITY OF MICHIGAN PRESS

Copyright © by the University of Michigan 1994
All rights reserved
Published in the United States of America by
The University of Michigan Press
Manufactured in the United States of America
⊖ Printed on acid-free paper

1997   1996   1995   1994   4   3   2   1

A CIP catalogue record for this book is available from the British Library.

Library of Congress Cataloging-in-Publication Data

Gilliom, John, 1960–
    Surveillance, privacy, and the law : employee drug testing and the
politics of social control / John Gilliom.
        p.   cm. — (Law, meaning, and violence)
    Includes bibliographical references and indexes.
    ISBN 0-472-10493-4
    1. Employees—Drug testing—United States. 2. Drug testing—Law
and legislation—United States. I. Title. II. Series.
HF5549.5.D7G55   1994
658.3'822—dc20   94-176
                                                                          CIP

Preface

When millions of American workers were subjected to dragnet policies of mandatory drug testing, the United States entered another battle in an ongoing war over surveillance and privacy. The Reagan administration and many of the nation's employers argued that testing was a necessary and effective method for dealing with a national drug crisis. Civil libertarians, union leaders, and many workers argued that testing was an unnecessary and invasive means of workplace surveillance. Like earlier fights over wiretapping, electronic eavesdropping, and lie detectors, this conflict almost immediately resulted in a burst of litigation over the issues of privacy, due process, and the Fourth Amendment.

This book studies the fight over employee drug testing. It has two main goals: to assess the nature of this new means of social control and to explain its rapid and largely successful deployment in the face of significant opposition. My work thus takes the form of two somewhat distinct narratives. One tells of drug testing as an innovative means of policing that is part of a broader move to bring social control policy toward an ideal of total surveillance and total crime prevention. While privacy and autonomy are the obvious casualties of such a system, it holds out the possibility of securing almost total compliance with the law in problematic areas like drug use, welfare administration, and taxation. In the fight over employee drug testing, then, we can study one moment in that broader movement and, perhaps, learn something about concurrent and future struggles.

The second narrative is less about testing than about the political and legal battles over its implementation. I seek to broaden our understanding of the politics of popular culture, ideological hegemony, and legal mobilization through an analysis of how employers, workers, lawyers, and judges struggled over this issue. We will see that the mass media's often fantastic imagery of a national drug crisis brought many Americans into full support for drug testing and other controversial antidrug policies. Others resisted the media barrage and voiced their opposition to testing. Using the language of law, they said: "We have rights and drug testing violates them." In a closely watched set of Supreme Court cases, however, a new conservative majority disagreed with that claim and gave a broad stamp of approval to the new policies. In the end, therefore, opposition to testing that had not been silenced by the threat of the drug crisis was contained and then silenced by the courts.

A project such as this one can never really be complete, and I do not claim to have exhausted the topics at hand. There is more research to be done in all the diverse manifestations of law and its controversies—tort law, labor law litigation and arbitration, and popular legal consciousness, to name a few key areas. And there is more to be done on the changing face of social control policy as we see innovations like computer matching, DNA typing, and other aspects of the contemporary revolution in surveillance technology. The goal here is to take a look at some of the core elements of this conflict—the drug warriors, the workers, the technology, and the federal courts—to begin a process of understanding the new state-citizen relationship and how it will unfold.

This project would not have taken shape without the help of Stuart Scheingold and Michael McCann—thanks to them for the help and for getting me started in a line of work that I enjoy very much. Don McCrone, Peter May, Lance Bennett, Ron Judd, and Stephen Majeski provided critical assistance on specific parts of the manuscript. Portions of this work appeared in the Summer 1992 issue of *Polity*, and my thanks go out to the anonymous reviewers for their contributions. Helena Silverstein, Austin Sarat, and Martha Minow each took on the invaluable task of reading the entire manuscript and letting me know where to add a bit, where to cut a bit, and where to make changes that went well beyond "a bit."

My colleagues in the Department of Political Science at Ohio University provided a welcoming and supportive environment in which to complete this project. Special thanks to Tom Walker and Gary Hawes for their generous counsel on both writing and farming.

Last in the list, but foremost in my thoughts, is Amy King. The initial idea for the project grew out of her work in information science, and she was a constant source of inspiration and support. For all of that and more, my thanks, my love, and my dedication.

Contents

Chapter 1

Surveillance, Hegemony, and the Law: Drug Testing in the American Workplace

In the 1980s, Americans heard that the nation faced a crisis of illegal drug use and were called to arms in a national "War on Drugs." We appointed a federal "Drug Czar" who thought it would be morally plausible to decapitate major dealers. We assigned the military to drug control activities, relaxed our search and seizure laws, enacted mandatory sentencing, and jailed a larger part of our population than any other nation on earth. In its overall impact, the War on Drugs marked a massive intensification in the government's ability to watch, control, and punish its citizens.

One key strategy of the war was to demand that American workers prove their abstinence from illegal drugs by urinating into small plastic bottles. This procedure came to be known as employee drug testing. As a technique of surveillance and control, the regular use of drug tests enables a new medical gendarme to observe and manage the behavior of individuals wherever they go and whenever they go there. The new techniques for analyzing the molecular properties of urine transform the body and its fluids into a veritable registry of the substances that a person has eaten, breathed, snorted, injected, or smoked. The result is that government and corporate authorities no longer need to discover misbehavior through verbal testimony or chance observation because they can cut through the human faculties of secrecy, deception, or denial, look inside the body, and see what the individual has been doing.

At the same time that drug-testing technology allows more intense and invasive scrutiny of the individual's life and body, its deployment in the workplaces of America broadly extends the reach and pervasiveness of the new mechanism of control. The workplace is, after all, an encompassing and critical part of American lives; it is where we spend most of our waking hours, draw our paychecks, obtain our medical insurance, and, for the fortunate, pursue a craft or profession that is of some personal reward. By implementing testing in the workplace, this new surveillance ability maximizes the exposure of citizens at the same time that it makes the penalties of even minor infraction immense.

Employee drug testing advances an approach to law and order that sees pervasive surveillance and control as a necessary and desirable part of modern governance. In this sense, it is part of a broader reorientation of social control policy encompassing such things as computer matching to detect financial misconduct (Reichman 1987), drunk driver checkpoints, video monitoring in banks and shopping malls, and the use of widespread surveillance as a general mechanism to control crime and deviance (Cohen 1985; Marx 1986; Rule et. al 1980). Together, these policies are part of a disciplining of social control that requires "permanent, exhaustive, omnipresent surveillance [that is] capable of making all visible" (Foucault 1979, 214).

But the idea of permanent and exhaustive surveillance bothers a lot of people. Indeed, workers facing drug testing have widely complained about the violation of privacy and dignity manifest in these programs. As one skilled blue collar worker surveyed in this project put it,

> It is an invasion of privacy, unconstitutional, and an OK to open the door to true programming of people and their private lives.

Another:

> Although I strongly oppose illegal drugs and agree something must be done, I feel this is a criminal problem. Testing for all is a further loss of rights and [brings] humiliation, mistakes and abuse for those who live within the law. I cannot accept any promise that this will not happen.

These workers are joined by many others in arguing that employee drug testing represents a significant and controversial change in the organization of social control in the United States. It creates a standing system of surveillance on mass populations and brings a new and empowering police role for employers. In doing so, it fundamentally challenges our conceptions of privacy, dignity, and due process of law. Why, then, did drug testing spread so rapidly and with apparently limited and largely unsuccessful opposition?

This book attempts to provide an answer. The pages and chapters that follow suggest that much of the potential opposition to drug testing never emerged because the imagery of a national drug crisis created a context in which people felt that drastic measures were needed to fight an apparently rampant epidemic of illegal drug use. The image of crisis in the popular culture—which was based on some truth and much illusion—served to preempt opposition by generating a broad wave of consent to and even active support for drug testing and related policy changes.

But opposition did take place. As members of our political culture and consumers of our mass media, workers in America largely accepted the imagery of the drug crisis. But many of these same people opposed testing policies because they felt that it violated their legal rights to privacy and due process. This opposition took the form of hundreds of lawsuits seeking to block testing and thus presented a significant challenge to the surveillance initiative.

In this way, the language of legal rights and the institutions of the legal system provided a seemingly promising counterargument and terrain of action for those who wanted to oppose this change in social control policy. But how well was that promise carried out? Past studies of the use of legal rights by opposition movements have suggested that rights claims are, at best, potentially valuable resources in broad campaigns (Scheingold 1974). At worst, they are a dead-end strategy that saps resources and frustrates the real interests of participants (Rosenberg 1991). Some students of law and politics even argue that the turn to rights is such a costly, alienating, and unsuccessful strategy that it should be avoided (Tushnet 1984).

But the turn to rights did look promising in this case: the liberal individualistic claims to privacy and due process, in the abstract, do a good job of expressing key facets of the opposition to testing. However, rights, of course, do not meaningfully exist in the abstract. As they take on practical meaning, they become a contingent part of real-life political, social, and legal conditions and struggles.

In the late 1980s, these conditions and struggles included the pervasive sense of a national drug crisis as well as the predominance of new conservative appointments to the federal courts. These judges and justices were increasingly rejecting older notions of individual rights in favor of a new perspective that works to augment and support surveillance and control programs like drug testing. In the process of dismissing the key arguments against testing, judges put forth a new framework for thinking about the relationship between the individual, the state, and its mechanisms of control. The ascendancy of this framework, it will be argued, virtually ensures that opposition to surveillance programs will find little support in the present judicial climate.

Thus the challenge to testing was contained: the turn to rights and legal action may have provided a course for opposition to take, but it also provided a system of language, political power, and institutional dynamics that can and did work to largely subvert oppositional claims. That is not to say that the turn to rights did not provide some important resources and rewards. The accuracy and procedural fairness of many programs were clearly improved by the threat or reality of legal action. Further, some unknown number of employers were scared away from testing by the possibility of a costly lawsuit (Axel 1991). But as for the fundamental critique of testing as an invasion of privacy and dignity, the law declared by the judges has not served workers well.

In exploring, detailing, and qualifying these arguments, this book will chart the social construction of the drug crisis of the 1980s to understand the origin and context of the testing movement and its popular support; explain the battle over drug testing in light of the economic and cultural dynamics behind both the bid to control and the bid to resist; explore the views of workers facing testing programs to understand how they feel and why they feel that way; and evaluate the role of the courts and the legal discourse of rights in shaping, expressing, and, in the end, defeating the claims of those who oppose testing.

The remainder of this introductory chapter provides a brief overview of the controversies surrounding testing policies to show that there is good reason to wonder how testing moved so easily into our lives. It then lays out the theoretical framework behind my exploration of how dynamics in the popular and legal cultures worked to preempt and limit potential opposition.

Drugs and Drug Tests

> Since Galen had taught that urine was secreted directly from the vena cava, and that its composition was a direct indication of the nature of the blood, doctors had tasted and smelled urine and had assayed it by the light of both sun and moon. The 16th century alchemists had learned to measure specific gravity with considerable precision and they subjected the urine of the sick to their methods. (Illich 1976, 161)

Having improved on the early urinalysis efforts of pioneers like Hippocrates and Galen,[1] contemporary physicians now study human urine as a guide to internal conditions like pregnancy, sugar imbalances, and a host of other medical conditions. In the wake of this medical success, the ability of urinalysis to reveal the chemistry of the body has led to its use in another area: government and corporate campaigns to stop people from using illegal drugs.

Beginning in the 1960s and early 1970s, urinalysis was used in the military, in prisons, and in drug rehabilitation programs. In the early 1980s, the navy undertook an ambitious testing program (Mulloy 1991), which was followed by pilot programs in a small number of corporations (Walsh and Trumble 1991). But it was not until the mid-1980s that testing became more widespread.[2] In 1986, President Ronald Reagan declared a national crusade against drug use and called for the testing of millions of American workers. Corporations, schools, and local governments soon moved to order drug testing for the people who fell under their administrative power. Within a few short years, more than half of the nation's largest employers were testing, and employers with testing programs encompassed roughly 20 percent of the work force (Greenberg, 1990; Zimmer and Jacobs 1992). In just a few short years, then, this major change in social control policy has been developed, implemented, and made a largely routine part of the workday in many professions.

Advocates of testing have portrayed the American work force as crumbling under the impact of illegal drugs and cast urine testing as a technological white knight that has arrived to save us. But critics have focused on a series of problems and flaws in testing programs and the rationales behind them; taken separately or as a whole, these clearly suggest that testing should be looked at with a skeptical eye. In relation to the larger argument of this book, these critiques are briefly previewed here to show that opposition to testing should or could have been both widespread and successful.

Privacy

> Suitable drug testing meant being forced by a nurse to drop her pants to her ankles, bend over at the waist with her knees slightly bent, hold her right arm in the air, and with her left hand angle a specimen bottle between her legs. She sobbed and shook, wet herself, and vomited. She was fired for insubordination: refusal to take another test. (Weiss 1986)[3]

The humiliation of compelled and often observed urination, the ability to probe and control an individual's behavior around-the-clock, and the access to medical information having nothing to do with illegal drugs have all been cited as intolerable aspects of drug-testing technologies. As Justice Scalia wrote in his dissent to *National Treasury Employees Union v. von Raab*, in which urination was not visually observed, "It is obvious that this is a type of search particularly destructive of privacy and offensive to personal dignity" (489 U.S. at 680).

Misdiagnosis

Reason suggests that if we are to expend the money and time to intrude on millions of Americans with mandatory workplace urinalysis, it should first be made clear that drug use is having a serious impact on the job. While we have all seen headline grabbing instances of troubled individuals and tragic accidents, impressions of an epidemic of workplace drug use appear to be unfounded. Indeed, Arthur McBay, chief toxicologist in the North Carolina medical examiner's office, has concluded,

> Advocates of drug testing have produced no evidence that there is a significant problem with drugs other than alcohol in the workplace, schools, and armed services, or that testing will have a major impact on the problem. (1987, 648)

While this may be a bit of an exaggeration, it is the case that drug-testing programs have had the ironic effect of revealing far less illegal drug use among American workers than advocates of testing had estimated. Some reports have found positive rates of up to 8 or 9 percent in programs that primarily test workers who are suspected of drug use (meaning that roughly 8 or 9 percent of *suspected* workers, not all workers, test positive). Large government programs of random testing have found less than 1 percent of workers testing positive for illegal drug use.[4] Along with the reassessment of the extent of drug use has come a reassessment of the impact of that drug use. New research has shown that early and highly publicized claims about the immense impact of drug use on work-place productivity and safety were incorrect and grossly exaggerated (see chap. 3; Morgan 1987; Zwerling, Ryan, and Orav 1990).

The impression of a national drug crisis and widespread threats to workplace safety are the central factors in understanding workers' support for drug-testing programs (see chap. 4). It is therefore essential to closely examine the nature of these threats. To challenge the prevailing beliefs about drug use in the workplace is not to suggest that there are no impaired workers or no workplaces that have particularly acute problems. It is, rather, to suggest that public and legal debate may be taking place under the influence of poorly derived, grossly inflated, or at least badly misdirected premises about the extent and nature of the problems we face.

Accuracy

Accuracy is a very complex issue in the politics of drug testing. Procedures and techniques change; the quality of testing laboratories varies; different workplaces use different programs, techniques, and detection levels. Finally, while some of us will be satisfied with a rate of, say, 93 percent accuracy, others will insist on 98 percent, and still others will demand the unreachable 100 percent guarantee that test results are correct.[5]

Early testing programs in the navy were so notoriously inaccurate that thousands of test results were called into question and more than 1,000 discharges reversed (*Los Angeles Times*, October 27, 1986). But contemporary programs that follow the Department of Health and Human Service's "Mandatory Guidelines for Federal Workplace

Drug Testing Programs" can be very accurate. Even so, as explained in chapter 3, error is an inescapable part of any drug-testing program. The inexpensive Enzyme Immunoassay Technique (EMIT)[6] test used by many employers as a screen test[7]—or as the sole test for many unfortunate job applicants—will be mistaken in somewhere from 5 to 38 percent of cases (Morgan 1987). In higher quality programs, positive findings on an EMIT or other screening test are confirmed using the very expensive Gas Chromatography/Mass Spectrometer (GC/MS) method, which is 100 percent accurate when all laboratory conditions and operator decisions are flawless. Given exceptionally stringent requirements for sample preparation and equipment cleaning, some authorities argue that even this best technique will be wrong in 3 to 5 percent of the cases because of contamination and error (see Morgan 1987, 14).

An early and authoritative study by the Centers for Disease Control found that *90 percent* of testing laboratories were below acceptable rates for the accurate detection of drugs such as morphine, barbiturates, amphetamines, and cocaine (Hansen, Caudill, and Boone 1985). By the late 1980s, however, the accuracy of testing had improved: "A study of 31 labs by the American Association of Clinical Chemists found no false positives and only 3% false negatives" (Zimmer and Jacobs 1992, 10). However, concerns remain that, given a high demand for testing services, these top laboratories are overworked, and cheaper, lower quality laboratories continue to pick up a sizable chunk of the market.

Since the tests essentially serve as witness, judge, and jury in putting people on trial for the use of illegal drugs, their technical reliability is critical. While error rates can be brought down to a tiny level with expensive replication and verification, the ever-present specters of human error, cost cutting, and the imperfections of science mean that mistakes will always be made. When even a small rate of error is spread over millions of people, many falsely ruined careers are the inevitable result.

Measuring Impairment

Pharmacologists and forensic scientists have repeatedly pointed out that current tests are simply unable to determine whether or not a person is under the influence of drugs, when drugs may have been used, or how much of a drug was taken (Dubowski 1987). In short, drug tests do not measure what should actually interest employers: on-the-job impairment. What most tests do measure are metabolites, chemical compounds that appear in the urine for some time after either drug use or its mental and physical effects have taken place. Metabolites are a poor indicator of the time or degree of drug use because individuals vary in the rate at which they process them (see Cornish 1988; Dubowski 1987). Since both the generation of metabolites and the generation of urine vary both with individuals and circumstance (e.g., heavy water consumption or exercise), there is no known way to establish a urine-based measure of the recency or intensity of drug use.

Each of these concerns—and others—will be addressed at greater length in the work that follows. This brief introduction to the many controversies surrounding the necessity, efficacy, fairness, and invasiveness of testing programs is provided here to show that this is no simple and straightforward case of meeting a clear public problem with an effective and reasonable policy response that should be embraced by American workers. If the testing movement is marked by so many technical shortcomings, flawed arguments, and burdensome impositions, why did it move so easily into the daily lives of American workers?

Hegemony and the Law

The Manufacture of Consent

The work of the Italian activist and theorist Antonio Gramsci has been a central part of many recent efforts to understand the dynamics of both political conflict and the absence of conflict over apparently contentious issues (Gaventa 1980; Gitlin 1980; Gramsci 1985; Hall et al. 1978; Scheingold 1989; Scott 1985). In explaining the organization of political and economic power in modern society, Gramsci stressed the need to see two overlapping but distinguishable ways, or "levels," through which preponderant groups maintain and exercise their power.

The first was "direct domination," which was costly and becoming less apparent in Western capitalist societies. "Direct domination," in Gramsci's formulation, is "the apparatus of state coercive power which 'legally' enforces discipline on those groups who do not 'consent' either actively or passively" (1985, 12). The second was ideological "hegemony," which comprises "the 'spontaneous' consent given by the great masses of the population to the general direction imposed on social life by the dominant fundamental group" (Gramsci 1985, 12; see the discussions in Gitlin 1980, 252–58; Hall 1979).

Authors working from a number of different perspectives have addressed concerns similar to those raised by the concept of ideological hegemony (Bennett 1980; Cobb and Elder 1975; Edelman 1967). Those works—and this one—deal with political conflicts that may seem a bit more mundane than the potential revolutions that were the subject of Gramsci's writings. However, their approach to the study of opinion, action, and power is quite similar. From this perspective, opinions and choices such as workers' responses to drug testing are shaped by the flow of ideas, information, and symbols in the popular culture. As Lance Bennett argues,

> Popular reactions to issues often depend on how the ideas and consequences are symbolized by elites, special interest organizations, and reference groups. . . . The way in which an issue is defined and presented to the public can affect the intensity, distribution, and expression of opinion. (1980, 248, 273)

This perspective does not share the assumptions of classical democratic theorists, who hold that people's opinions emerge from autonomous experience, stable values, and reasoned analysis. Rather, perceptions and opinions are formed through the consumption of mass media news and political imagery. The main thrust of this orientation is that we should think of "the 'spontaneous' consent given by the great masses" as not being all that spontaneous (as Gramsci's quotation marks suggest). Rather, consent to impositions or adverse conditions may be the result of actions taken by elites and systemic "biases" that favor their interests (Schattschneider 1960).

In *Power and Powerlessness* (1980), John Gaventa argues that he has identified a setting that is almost entirely under the grips of ideological hegemony (as well as other forms of power). In the small coal-mining town he studies, subjugated people do not even perceive the necessity for resisting some key dimensions of their own domination. Gaventa argues that this failure to recognize political problems is the result of ideological hegemony (Gaventa 1980, 13). The powers exercised in this setting include

> the means through which power influences, shapes or deter-
> mines conceptions of the necessities, possibilities, and strategies
> of challenge in situations of latent conflict. [Efforts to understand
> this process] may include the study of social myths, language,
> and symbols, and how they are shaped and manipulated in
> power processes. It may involve the study of communication of
> information—both of what is communicated and how it is done.
> (Gaventa 1980, 15)[8]

James Scott (1985), on the other hand, argues that the idea of ideological hegemony may be a myth, that dominated groups do maintain counterhegemonic discourses and terms of resistance. Scott studied the question of ideological hegemony through an analysis of whether or not peasants actually consent to their own exploitation. He found that members of a Malaysian village who were being displaced by economic and technological change had, in their own traditional terms, a critical discourse with which they could address both their problems and the people behind them. Finding that the peasants did have an active counterhegemonic discourse, Scott argued that to understand their compliant behavior, we should not assume ideological consent. Rather, he argued, the villagers more likely went through a "grudging resignation" to their plight (Scott 1985, 325).

> Compliance can of course flow either from grudging resignation
> or from active ideological support. What we should not do, how-
> ever, is to infer ideological support from the most apparently
> faithful compliance. To prove the case for ideological support—
> for hegemony—one would have to supply independent evidence
> that the values of the subordinate class are in fact largely in
> accord with those of the dominant elite. Such evidence, to be
> credible, would have to come from social contexts in which mem-
> bers of the subordinate class were least constrained by power
> relations. (Scott 1985, 325)

Workers who show not just "grudging compliance" to but active support for drug testing might, therefore, be said to be undergoing some form of ideological hegemony. Roughly half of the more than eight hundred skilled workers surveyed in chapter 4 support testing. In light of the preceding critiques showing that the testing initiative is fraught with problems and drawbacks for workers, how do we best explain this support?

As explained in chapter 2, drug testing emerged in the context of a widely touted war against a national drug crisis. Americans who followed television news, newspapers, or the weekly magazines were repeatedly told that the nation was crumbling under the impact of illegal drug use. While only partly true, this imagery of crisis worked to create a social context that was widely receptive to drug testing and other "antidrug" policies. In this way, as Edelman and Hall have argued, social crises help elites generate consent among the mass public. In doing so, potential conflict is avoided as people applaud rather than protest policies that they might oppose in the absence of a crisis mentality.

But the research presented in chapter 4 shows that the influence of the crisis mentality is partially constrained by other factors in the popular culture. While workers' assessments of the national drug problem were significantly related to their positions on testing, other factors had an even stronger relationship. Foremost among these was whether they felt that testing violated legal rights to privacy. Many workers who felt that the United States was facing a drug crisis still opposed testing and, in most cases, cited their legal rights as the reason for opposing it. Attorneys for labor organizations and civil liberties groups relied on these same rights claims in filing hundreds of lawsuits in opposition to workplace testing.

The Containment of Opposition

[Hegemony] does not just passively exist as a form of dominance. It has continually to be renewed, recreated, defended, and modified. It is also continually resisted, limited, altered, challenged by pressures not all its own. (Williams 1977, 112)

Resistance and challenge are a likely part of any hegemonic system. The challenge to testing is not, of course, action on the revolutionary scale that Gramsci had hoped for. Indeed, only about 2 percent of the antitesting workers met in chapter 4 express themselves in explicitly class-conscious terms. The vast majority use the well-known terms of their liberal culture and build their opposition to drug testing around legal rights claims.

This opposition is a form of resistance or challenge to the system that produced the testing initiative. As Scott defined it, the concept of resistance refers to "any act(s) by member(s) of a subordinate class that is or are *intended* either to mitigate or deny claims . . . made on that class by superordinate classes . . . or to advance its own claims . . . vis-à-vis those superordinate classes" (Scott 1985, 290, emphasis in the original; see Genovese 1972).[9] But the nature of this resistance effort raises the question whether demands that *do* reflect the dominant ideology of liberal legalism can be effective for those who rely on them (Williams 1977, 114; see also Foucault 1980b, 108). In short, can resistance really be a meaningful challenge if it is advanced in the formal legal terms of the state?

By framing opposition in legal terms, workers opposed to testing gained a shared language, some apparent rhetorical clout, the help of the American Civil Liberties Union (ACLU), and a promising and accessible venue of conflict. With favorable legal opinions, they would have the leverage to force employers to respect their demands. Thus, by using the terms of law, workers appear to gain a great deal.

But many scholars see the law and the courts as a means of preserving, not changing, prevailing economic and political relations. They see it, in short, as an integral part of a hegemonic process, not an escape from it (see Greer 1982; Kairys 1982). Gramsci himself expressed great cynicism about the liberating potential of law, when he wrote (from his prison cell) that "the Law is the repressive and negative aspect of the entire positive, civilising activity undertaken by the State" (1985, 246-47). Obviously, Gramsci would not have seen a rights claim and subsequent litigation as a meaningful or promising form of popular resistance.

Some contemporary scholars argue that the law cannot be counterhegemonic because the very ideological "form" of law (Hunt 1985) precludes its successful use by those challenging the dominant order. The law's primary organizing ideas, such as individualism, private property, equal opportunity, and sometimes the very idea of a "right," they argue, are fundamental obstacles to the expression and realization of the goals sought by opposition movements (see Freeman 1982; Tushnet 1984; see the discussions in Crenshaw 1988; McCann 1989; Scheingold 1989; Silverstein and Van Dyk 1989).

On the topic of drug testing, one could say that claims to privacy rights are a bad move for workers because these claims come from and support a liberal capitalist matrix of selfish individualism and private property. Since selfish individualism and private property are seen by many as long-term enemies of a successful labor movement, the ideology of law is, ipso facto, a losing proposition for workers.

One could also argue that the necessary abstraction of a rights claim distorts the real issues and masks what workers really feel. The complaint should not be, "This violates my right to privacy," but, rather, "I will not pee in a jar so that you can analyze my life," or as one worker put it, "It is a degradation of the human spirit, damn you!" As Tushnet argued,

> It is a form of alienation or reification to characterize this as an instance of "exercising my rights." We must insist on preserving real experiences rather than abstracting general rights from those experiences. The language of rights should be abandoned to the very great extent that it takes as a goal the realization of the reified abstraction "rights" .... (1984, 1382)

But others have argued that rights claims are often the most appropriate and effective means available for the mobilization of resistance in this society (Crenshaw 1988). Both intellectual and popular cultures in the United States retain a good deal of faith in the powerful appeal of the law (Merry 1986; Milner 1989; see also McCann 1986, 106–21; Scheingold 1974).[10] Duncan Kennedy uncharacteristically expressed these sentiments when he wrote,

> Embedded in the rights notion, is a liberating accomplishment of our culture: the affirmation of free human subjectivity against the constraints of group life, along with the paradoxical countervision of a group life that creates and nurtures individuals capable of freedom. (1981, 506)

Along with this faith in the law is a point made clear in Kimberle Crenshaw's observation that there may be no feasible alternative to the dominant ideology of law:

Popular struggles are a reflection of institutionally determined logic and a challenge to that logic. People can only demand change in ways that reflect the logic of the institutions that they are challenging. Demands for change that do not reflect the institutional logic—that is, demands that do not engage and subsequently reinforce the dominant ideology—will probably be ineffective. (1988, 1367; see also Scott 1985)

The conundrum facing students of legal politics is well expressed in some widely cited lines from E. P. Thompson's *Whigs and Hunters: The Origins of the Black Act*. Law is, of course, primarily constructed and controlled by elites, but as a code and ideology it also holds the possibility of constraining elites' ability to exercise their power in capricious or unjust ways:

On the one hand, it is true that the law did mediate existent class relations to the advantage of rulers . . . . On the other hand, the law mediated these class relations through legal forms which imposed, again and again, inhibitions on the actions of the rulers. . . . And not only were the rulers (indeed, the ruling class as a whole) inhibited by their own rules of law against the exercise of direct unmediated force . . . but they also believed enough in these rules and the accompanying ideological rhetoric, to allow, in certain limited areas, the law itself to be a genuine forum in which certain kinds of class conflict were fought out. (Thompson 1975, 264–65)

The debate over the possibilities and limits of legal action is central and undying in the field (see, for example, McCann 1986, 1994; Rosenberg 1991; Scheingold 1989). A study such as this book can only hope to contribute to the debate by offering one more cut on how the constraints and resources of law play out in a particular social and political conflict. My analysis of legal disputes in the cases studied here suggests that the ideological terrain or form of American law does offer the possibility for the effective use of legal claims in resisting drug testing. Legal values of privacy and due process as well as Fourth Amendment limits on searches are not ideal expressions of workers' views, but they do reflect and express their concerns to a strong degree.

But finding a home—albeit imperfect—in legal ideology is no guarantee that one's complaints will be heard and acted on. The ideology of law is both open-ended and contingent. That is, the terms of legal discourse can be used to make numerous and contradictory arguments, and they take on real meaning only as they are put to work in our political and social lives. Therefore, it is necessary to study not just the ideology of law but the political and institutional processes that make law—law as it is struggled over by interest groups, lawyers, and judges and enforced (or not enforced) by political institutions (Galanter 1974; McCann 1986; see Goldman and Sarat 1989).

Does the legal process fulfill its promise in the cases at hand? No. Opinions in leading federal cases show that there is widespread disagreement and confusion in the judicial response to these conflicts. Some judges have marshaled strong arguments against drug testing based on privacy, due process, and the Fourth Amendment. Had these opinions prevailed, the testing initiative would have been dealt a massive setback. But in the influential Supreme Court rulings on suspicionless drug testing, we witness a broad defeat for opponents of testing. Not only did the Court discount or reject a number of important complaints put forth by workers, but it relied on an ideology of social control that appears to negate the very rights claims on which antitesting arguments rely.

The ideology of law, therefore, contains the terms to resist testing, but the political process of breathing meaning into vague ideological terms works against it. In this way, the counterhegemonic potential of law discussed by Thompson has been unrealized: the main impact of the law in these cases is to constrain and discount the opposition. Having lost in court, workers who refuse to take drug tests most often face termination (see Cornish 1988, 243–44). This threat of lost income and benefits, then, brings forth the coercive face of political and economic domination that one anticipates when the more gentle forms of cultural and legal domination break down (Gramsci 1985, 12).

Chapter 2

The Social Construction
of a Drug Crisis

The drug crisis is a crisis of authority.

—William Bennett, 1989

There is of course no simple consensus, even here, as to the nature, causes and extent of the crisis. But the over-all tendency is for the way the crisis has been ideologically constructed in the dominant ideologies to win consent in the media, and thus to constitute the substantive basis in "reality" to which public opinion continually refers. In this way, by "consenting" to the view of the crisis which has won credibility in the echelons of power, popular consciousness is also won to support . . . the measures of control and containment which this version of social reality entails. (Hall et al. 1978, 220–21)

The controversy over employee drug testing is inseparable from the broader intensification of the society's focus on illegal drugs in the mid-1980s. President Reagan cited a national drug crisis and the apparent failure of traditional methods of drug-supply interdiction in calling for widespread random urinalysis. Judges, employers, and workers themselves point to the crisis in explaining the need for testing. This chapter, therefore, is less about drug testing itself than it is about the drug crisis and the broader social and political climate that supports the testing movement.

Our focus turns to these issues for two reasons. First, an explanation of the momentum behind the testing movement must begin with an analysis of the many values and interests that combined to propel these and similar policies in the 1980s. Second, in answering questions about the consent of workers faced by testing programs and the shaping of legal conflict over testing, it is necessary to understand the origins of the crisis mentality. As will be seen in chapter 4, workers who feel that we face a national drug crisis are significantly more likely to support drug testing than those who do not. The specter of the drug crisis, in short, is a crucial part of understanding both the origin and legitimation of drug testing.

The Politics of Social Problems

At any one time, a wide range of ambiguous social problems exists for society to deal with. Poverty, health care, pollution, foreign powers, street crime, drug use, declining privacy, runaway corporate power, political corruption and incompetence, or budget deficits could each be the center of attention in contemporary American politics. Yet during different periods, different problems draw the attention of officials and publics. Why did the general issue of illegal drug use and the specific issue of workplace drug use emerge as central social issues of the 1980s? Why was the drug crisis framed by so many as, in Mr. Bennett's terms, "a crisis of authority"?

The need to study the politics of social problems and proffered solutions is well expressed by Murray Edelman:

> Problems come into discourse and therefore into existence as reinforcements of ideologies, not simply because they are there or because they are important for well-being. They signify who are virtuous and useful and who are dangerous and inadequate, which actions will be rewarded and which penalized. They constitute people as subjects with particular kinds of aspirations, self-concepts and fears, and they create beliefs about the relative importance of events and objects. They are critical in determining who exercise authority and who accept it. (1988, 12, emphasis added; see also Gusfield 1963, 1981; Hall et al. 1978)

Edelman reminds us that social problems are constructed, not discovered, and that they both emerge from and advance given ideologies and systems of power. Following this suggestion, it is necessary to examine the intertwining of ideology, interest, and power manifest in the construction of social problems and policies.[1]

Stuart Hall and his colleagues followed this route in analyzing the alleged mugging crisis that occurred in the United Kingdom in the early 1970s. In *Policing the Crisis* (1978), these authors show that it was the police who provided the press and public with the frightening new term *mugging* as well as the statistics that showed a spree of such crimes. After analyzing the social history of the crisis, they argue that the mugging threat had been exaggerated and that its centrality within social discourse was in large part tied to its role in legitimating authoritarian state policies.

The mugging crisis allowed the reclassification of racial problems as street crime and won public consent to a draconian police crackdown and expansion of state power. Hence, in the wake of the politicized black protest and critique of police brutality in the 1960s, black youth were once again redefined as threatening and violent. Concomitantly, the police and judges were recast as protectors in need of both extensive support and latitude in the use of violence and harsh sentencing. Hall and his colleagues speculate that such crises and responses not only lead to the maintenance and further centralization of social control but that the very need for more authoritative control in declining capitalist societies helps fuel the definitions of the crises themselves.[2]

To call attention to the social construction of social problems is not to argue that these problems are without an element of reality (see Hall et al. 1978, 182–83). It would be foolish to argue either (1) that the United States is without a drug problem or (2) that a widespread and deeply felt sense of crisis could be sustained for a long period of time without having some basis in reality. By *construction*, rather, I mean the social process of centering public attention (which may include the exaggeration of threats), defining the problem, and prescribing "solutions."

To understand the construction of the drug crisis, it is necessary to account for the reality behind the crisis, but it may be even more important to analyze patterns of behavior in the mass media and among the politicians and interest groups that populate the public space in America. Among key elements in explaining the drug crisis of the 1980s are the ongoing existence and impact of illegal drug use; the characteristics and behavior of the mass media; the mobilization of a morally conservative political coalition; and the success of conservative "law and order" politicians in pushing an agenda of firm discipline and hierarchical social control. Each will be addressed in turn.

Illegal Drug Use in the 1980s

While journalists and government officials often speak quite confi-
dently about actual levels of drug use and abuse in the United States,
a careful look at the available concepts and measures shows little
reason for that confidence. The following pages take up three main
issues. First, the term *drug* is so vaguely and improperly used that
we can hardly even begin to talk about the drug problem without a
good deal of clarification. Second, available measures of illegal drug
use in the United States suffer from methodological shortcomings
that raise serious questions about their validity. Third, and perhaps
most surprisingly, it appears—using the most widely relied on of
these imperfect measures—that most forms of drug use in the United
States have been in decline since the late 1970s and early 1980s.

Drugs

In the American vernacular, *drug* refers to marijuana, cocaine, heroin, PCP (phencyclidine), hallucinogens, and a range of licit medications and other chemical compounds that are subject to abuse. In
both the vernacular and the public policy process, *drug* does not refer
to the widely abused and socially destructive substances alcohol and
tobacco.

Along with excluding key substances of abuse, the vernacular
term *drug*—as in *drug crisis* and *drug war*—collapses very important
distinctions between illegal drugs. From almost any perspective, it is
absurd to categorize cocaine, heroine, and marijuana together in a
lump category, yet that is precisely what we tend to do in trying to
discuss and assess the drug problem (Zimring and Hawkins 1992).
The most dramatic television news footage of the 1980s came from
crack cocaine, yet the widely touted statistics about the drug crisis in
America are built primarily on the larger population numbers related
to marijuana use. Unlike crack, marijuana is not addictive, is not
known to cause significant long-term health problems, does not create dangerous behavior patterns, and has not been linked to an out-
break of crime on the streets. As Zimring and Hawkins put it,

> From the standpoint of every significant social value except
> political compliance, marijuana is a relatively benign substance,

and a major campaign to reduce its use would not produce obvious or substantial benefits. (1992, 181)

Yet the vast majority of behavior covered under terms like *drug problem, drug crisis,* or *drug abuse* (and the vast majority of positive drug test results) are related solely to marijuana. The category of *drugs,* therefore, grafts the imagery of severe and addictive drugs used by a tiny minority onto the high use numbers produced by the "relatively benign" and widely used marijuana.

Measures and Trends

While all measures of drug use are flawed, the most widely relied on statistics in the nation are from the National Institute on Drug Abuse's (NIDA) regular surveys of American households and high school students.[3] These are the two sources "from which most of our knowledge about the use of illegal drugs in the United States is derived" (Morgan 1988, 688).[4] A look at the trends revealed in the NIDA household survey data on people's reported drug use within the month preceding the survey shows several important points that may be surprising to those who lived through the Drug Crisis of the 1980s.[5]

—Illegal drug use by young people has been on a downward trend since the late 1970s (NIDA 1990, 20–30). 1979 appears to be the peak year in the NIDA data with 35 percent of eighteen to twenty-five year olds reporting using marijuana and 9 percent reporting using cocaine in the month prior to the survey. By 1982 it was 27 percent for marijuana and 7 percent for cocaine. 1985 saw 22 percent for marijuana and 8 percent for cocaine, and 1988 saw 15.5 percent for marijuana and 4.5 percent for cocaine. Figures for twelve to seventeen year olds are much lower and follow the same basic pattern.
—Illicit drug use among adults aged twenty-six and over has been largely steady or declining during this period. In 1979, 6 percent reported marijuana use in the month prior to the survey, and 1 percent reported using cocaine. In 1982 it was 7 percent for marijuana and 1 percent for cocaine. 1985 saw 6

percent marijuana and 2 percent cocaine, and 1988 saw 4 percent marijuana and 1 percent cocaine.

—Marijuana is by far the most widely used illegal drug in America (NIDA 1990, 13), and reported annual use among the entire
population has been going down since—at the latest—1982.

In short, there was no nationwide burst in drug use in the 1980s
that can account for the eruption of attention and action in the circles
of media, government, and public opinion.[6] Actually, what occurred
was a broadly based decline in most forms of illegal drug use—a
decline that was under way before the War on Drugs even began.

The relationship between empirical evidence and the impression
of a drug crisis grows more tenuous when the impact of illegal drugs
is compared to other problems. It is exceedingly difficult to establish
a meaningful measurement of the health impact of widespread behaviors—issues of measurement, causality, and assessment seem to
confound any effort to get a clear picture of the situation. A recent
effort undertaken at Brandeis University[7] attempts to paint a rough
picture by, among other things, estimating the number of deaths
linked to substance abuse. Their data on mortality show that while
illegal drug use was an important problem in the 1980s, alcohol and
tobacco use were taking an even greater death toll on our society
(Robert Woods Johnson Foundation, 1993).

Basing their analysis on the Vital Statistics data of the U.S. National Center for Health Statistics, the researchers report that the late
1980s saw roughly ten thousand deaths per year that were directly
caused by illegal drug use. Deaths directly caused by alcohol use
ranged between seventeen and twenty thousand per year. There
were nearly 117,000 deaths attributed to lung cancer with ninety
percent of those caused by tobacco smoking. Now, in each case, there
are other deaths less directly related to these behaviors—some
300,000 are linked to smoking-related diseases other than lung-can-
cer, nearly 90,000 are indirectly linked to alcohol use. It is impossible
to ascertain how many deaths are indirectly linked to illegal drug
use, but we know that by the late 1980s, we approached nearly 8,000
AIDS deaths among intravenous drug users and their partners, and
there was, obviously, some number of deaths caused by traffic accidents and falls.[8]

It would be myth making to suggest that we have a firm understanding of the toll in these areas, but these figures do point to the conclusion that while illegal drug use was an important public health problem in the 1980s, it was surely not one justifying the hysteria devoted to it.

The points raised in the preceding pages suggest caution in the reception of claims about the impact of drug use on society and the workplace. When it comes down to it, we have only a general sense of what the real extent and nature of drug use is, but it appears to be down in recent years (see Zimring and Hawkins 1992, 23, 39). Further, when we unpack or deconstruct the term *drug*, we see that most drug use is marijuana use and that more notorious and dangerous substances like cocaine are not widely used: NIDA's 1990 study found 13 percent reporting marijuana use in the year prior to the survey and only 3 percent using cocaine. Less than 1 percent reported using cocaine in the month prior to the survey.

While there are some people for whom drug use becomes a problem, there does not seem to be a magnitude of crisis calling for the budget allocations, public attention, and draconian changes in American society that the War on Drugs has been associated with. As explained earlier, this is not to say that there are not significant problems surrounding illegal drug use. Rather, it is to say that the problems of illegal drug use are comparable to or smaller than a number of other problems that receive little if any attention and that fluctuations in drug use cannot account for the burst of political attention seen in the middle and late 1980s. Again, the intent here is not to belittle the illegal drug problem, but to raise questions about why this problem became *the* problem of the 1980s. Indeed, even if available data demonstrated a clear increase in drug use, we would still not have a sufficient explanation of the emergence of the drug crisis. Since a number of pressing social concerns exist at any one time, and only a few become "problems" or "crises" (Edelman, 1988), an explanation of a crisis episode must include more than an empirical demonstration of importance. How, then, do we explain the drug crisis and the war on drugs? Like any other social problem or issue, we must look at its social construction in the image-laden world of American politics and the mass media.

Journalists on Drugs

The spectacle constituted by news reporting continuously con-
structs and reconstructs social problems, crises, enemies, and leaders and so creates a succession of threats and reassurances. These
constructed problems and personalities furnish the content of political journalism and the data for historical and analytic political
studies. They also play a central role in winning support and opposition for political causes and policies.

—Murray Edelman

The place of the drug issue among the problems of society has been
exaggerated by the press. Trends in drug use have been misrepre-
sented. The impression that has been given is that the problem is
out of control and growing. That's simply not true.

—Ben Bagdikian

In a 1986 poll on drug abuse and attitudes, ABC News found that 84
percent of the public had heard of crack and that 73 percent of that
group could identify it as a type of cocaine. But only 4 percent
thought that they had personally seen someone selling crack, only 3
percent knew someone who had tried crack, and only 1 percent had
ever tried it themselves (ABC News 1986). Despite this dearth of
personal experience, some 54 percent said it would be very or fairly
easy to buy crack in their area. Seventy-six percent were willing to
say that the drug problem was bigger in 1986 than in 1981, and 62
percent said that it was a "great deal bigger". It was, by most measures, smaller.

These gaps between personal experience and the perception of
social reality emphasize the importance of recognizing the mediation
of experience in mass society. No matter what the actual magnitude
of a form of behavior in a mass society, especially one as secret as
illegal drug use will tend to be, it cannot be experienced by the public
without the help of the mass media (Bennett 1988; Scheingold 1984).
As Hall and his colleagues put it,

The mass media are not the only, but they are among the most
powerful forces in the shaping of public consciousness about
topical and controversial issues. The signification of events
within the mass media thus provides one key terrain where consent is won or lost. (1978, 220)

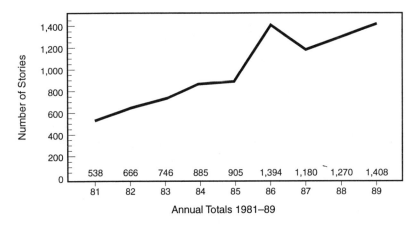

Fig. 1. News coverage of cocaine and marijuana in the *New York Times*, 1981–89. (*Source:* Original NEXIS search.)

There is, of course, no guarantee that the media image will be an accurate reflection of social trends. As has been exhaustively documented in sociological studies of mass media news making, news is not made and sustained unless politicians, officials, and other authorities participate by providing opinions, observations, and newsworthy activity (see generally Bennett 1988).[9] The pages that follow provide a brief overview of some of the central events and motivations involved in explaining the convergence of the politicians' and the mass media's attention to drug use.

There is no doubt that media coverage of illegal drugs skyrocketed in the mid-1980s. As seen in figure 1, a NEXIS search of the *New York Times* from 1981 to 1990 confirms that a dramatic pattern of escalation was occurring. In 1981, there were 538 stories that contained the words *cocaine* or *marijuana*. In 1982, it was up to 666. 1983 saw 746. 1984 saw 885. In 1985, it was up to 905. In 1986, a big year for both elections and the drug crisis, there were 1,394 stories in this category, but by 1987 things tapered off to 1,180. 1988 held steady at 1,270 stories while 1989 had 1,408. Clearly, the media and the society had turned their attention to illegal drugs. Oddly, our attention was turning as drug use went down.

1986—the year of President Reagan's speech calling for nationwide testing, the year of the drug-related deaths of the young athletes Len Bias and Don Rogers, the year of crack—was the year when the flow truly intensified. In the fall of 1985, the media pump began to be primed for the forthcoming burst of coverage on drugs. In October, Robert Stutman, a special agent for the Drug Enforcement Administration (DEA), was put in charge of the organization's New York office. While the previous administrators had worked more quietly, Stutman "quickly established good relations with CBS News, *The Times*, and other news organizations and worked to make his staff accessible to reporters" (Kerr 1986, 12). During that same time, *New York Times* editor A. M. Rosenthal was visited by the Reverend Jesse Jackson, and the two had a long discussion about drugs. Recalled Rosenthal, "I felt after Jesse's visit that we ought to be paying more attention to drugs than we were." In November 1985, the *Times* assigned a full-time reporter to the "drug beat."

At just this time, the new term *crack* entered the mass media in the text of a November 1985 *New York Times* story on a drug counseling center (Gladwell 1986). Cocaine—once a seemingly acceptable and even glamorized drug of movie stars and the white upper classes—had earned a new name as it had been refined into a cheaper and more powerful form and come into the hands of urban African-Americans. Within a year of that first mention, the major media had carried more than a thousand stories on crack and other addictive drugs; CBS's "48 Hours on Crack Street" had drawn fifteen million viewers, and the other networks produced a similar slate of dramatic accounts of the new crisis.[10]

In "I Was a Drug-Hype Junkie," Adam Weisman explains the magnetism of drug crisis news stories that seemed to inundate the press in the mid-1980s. "In a way, it was the perfect cover story: sensational, colorful, gruesome, alarmist, with a veneer of social responsibility. Unfortunately it just wasn't true" (1986, 15). In the preelection weeks of September 1986, the media coverage of the crack epidemic grew so intense that the DEA felt obliged to publicly announce that their studies showed that crack was not a widely prevalent drug; rather, it was seen as a secondary problem limited to some cities and neighborhoods. The *New York Times* and *Newsweek* ignored the announcement, *Time* magazine mentioned it in its "Press" segment, and the *Washington Post* placed it back on page 18 (Gladwell 1986, 10).

Newsweek magazine was one of the most excited clarions of the illegal drug issue and had no less than three cover stories on drugs within five months. Drug covers outsold regular issues by 10 to 35 percent. But maybe marketing strategies weren't the only concern here. *Newsweek* editor in chief Richard M. Smith said that "by now virtually every family had been affected by the drug crisis, or they knew somebody affected by it. As an editor, I felt the need to put the drug problem in a larger context than we had in the past" (Kerr 1986, 12).

Whatever Smith's feelings, his claim about affected families was absurd. A 1986 national poll by ABC found only 13 percent of respondents saying that drugs had ever caused a problem in their family; only 3 percent had problems "these days" (ABC News 1986). Thirty-one percent of respondents said they had a friend who used marijuana, and 17 percent had a friend who used cocaine. Drug use was obviously occurring, but the hyperbole of people like Smith was without credible foundation. Weisman points out that in relation to the drug story, credible foundations were of little importance in that there was no one who was going to correct media claims. While other issues often have pressure groups and politicians making claims and counterclaims, the drug issue was a one-sided affair.[11]

It was during what Arnold Trebach (1987) calls "the scared summer of 1986" that the highest levels of media attention were reached. On Sunday, May 18, three major New York papers—the *Times*, the *Daily News*, and *Newsday*—ran feature articles on crack. On June 16, *Newsweek* ran one of its most dramatic cover stories on the drug peril. Editor Smith equated drugs with medieval plagues and the attack on Pearl Harbor—the survival of the nation was at stake. Analysts have often pointed to a tendency toward dramatization in the news industry (Bennett 1988), and the drug story definitely fits this mold. Pictures of users and arrests filled the news, and *Time* magazine portrayed the United States as "a nation wrestl[ing] with the dark and dangerous recesses of its soul" (September 16, 1986, 56). Early in that same summer, two relatively well-known young athletes—Len Bias and Don Rogers—died while using cocaine. As Trebach puts it,

> Coming on top of all the previous hysteria, the tragic deaths of these two young Americans pushed the governmental and social leadership of the most powerful nation on earth into frenzied action in all directions at once. (1987, 7)

But despite these dramatic visions and personalized tragedies, Weisman (1986) points out that what *Newsweek* saw as a "plague" and *U.S. News and World Report* saw as the nation's "#1 menace" was simply not—as seen—a problem of those proportions. Weisman explains how reporters would approach ambiguous and approximate statistics and select the most alarming possible dimensions for inclusion in their stories. For example, if NIDA estimated that three to five million people had used cocaine in the previous thirty-day period, reporters would quote the higher figure and claim that there were at least five million regular users of cocaine in the country (Weisman 1986).

Malcolm Gladwell, writing for *Insight,* the magazine of the conservatively backed *Washington Times,* concludes that even though the press "hyped" the drug story and twisted statistics, the drug story was what the public wanted (1986, 11). Asserting that the media followed a public lead, Gladwell argues that public opinion polls show a swing in public attitudes toward drugs and that this is what the press coverage expressed. Citing David Musto's theory that the American public follows pendulumlike swings between libertarianism and authoritarianism, Gladwell argues that the public had swung to a position of authoritarian caution and that the drug hype and the broader War on Drugs was thus a grass roots movement that played its way from the people up through the media to the government. Another dimension of Musto's argument is cited by Kerr in a similar analysis of the drug coverage. Kerr notes that Musto expects there to be a lag in public response to a wave of drug abuse. Thus an epidemic that began in the 1960s only began to take a noticeable public toll by the 1980s. The result, it is argued, is that "the popular image of drugs becomes negative" (Kerr 1986, 12).

While these arguments seem intuitively plausible, there is a problem with the positing of some sort of coherent American public that has a massive, largely simultaneous, and clear-headed grass roots reckoning with the impact of drug use. Mass publics do not have simultaneous firsthand experiences; trends and problems like society-wide drug use, crime, and budget deficits are experienced through the eye of the mass media. Gladwell asserts that the media followed a public lead, but there is a major flaw in this argument: news making relies on credible, centralized, and usually official sources for constructing the news image (Bennett 1988; Sigal 1973).

Except in the delayed terms of audience shares and newsstand sales, the public has a very limited role in the construction of the news. Therefore, it is essential to go behind the media coverage to explore changes among influential political forces in the United States.

The Crisis Coalition

The Reagan White House was a welcome home for the moralistic anticrime politics of the drug crisis and the purported "war" to save the nation. The Reagan coalition incorporated a religious fundamentalism that fixated on drug use as a story of permissiveness and moral decline and a law and order mentality that was looking for an excuse to "get tough on crime." These elements combined with the more immediate political interests of the administration and led the Reagans to sponsor one of the greatest social frenzies and draconian police crackdowns in recent history.

Early 1981 was a "honeymoon" period for the Reagans in almost every respect, but by the latter months of the year the administration faced several public relations problems. By the time the federal budget proposal was released in February of 1982—in the face of rising unemployment and budget director Stockman's revelations that much of the "supply-side" strategy was a sham—there was widely expressed concern over the fairness of the Reagan agenda (see Hertsgaard 1988, 158–59).

Public opinion polls suggested that Nancy Reagan was increasingly seen as a Marie Antoinette who partied with the wealthy and aspired to little more than expensive china and designer gowns (Hertsgaard 1988, 158–59). In the period from November 1981 to February 1982, the White House staff apparently developed a consensus that the drug problem would provide a more useful and politically resonant issue for the first lady than her soon-to-be-forgotten Foster Grandparents Program. Soon Mrs. Reagan was widely seen meeting with concerned parents, attending drug abuse conferences and counseling centers, and urging children to "just say no."[12] Once her national Just Say No campaign was under way, writers for the *New York Times* and the *Washington Post* report that senior management made it clear that Nancy Reagan was no longer a safe target for cynical news coverage (see Hertsgaard 1988, 156–59; Trebach 1987, 134–35).

Mrs. Reagan's Just Say No campaign was widely criticized by treatment experts for being overly simplistic and naive about the cause and treatment of addictive drug use. Nonetheless, the politically successful campaign was continued throughout the 1980s. The Reagans' broader focus on illegal drugs continued with varying intensity through the middle years of the decade, but it was in 1986, with the events and media coverage discussed earlier, the approach of a crucial congressional election, and increasing problems over its foreign policies, that the administration's attention to illegal drugs in America skyrocketed.[13]

On September 14—just as *Time* magazine was running its drug crisis cover story about a nation "wrestl[ing] with the dark and dangerous recesses of its soul"—President and Mrs. Reagan went on national television to talk to the "American family" about drugs. "Drugs are menacing our society. They're threatening our values and undercutting our institutions." Drawing upon images of the Normandy invasion and the courage of Lincoln, they introduced a war on drugs and asked, "Won't you join us in this great, new, national campaign?" On the next day, September 15, President Reagan issued an executive order calling for a drug free federal workplace and ordering the mandatory random urine testing of as many as 1.2 million federal employees.[14]

It is not even worth belaboring the point that political hay can be made from the issue of illegal drugs. The topic involves the drama, public enemies, and moralistic veneer that go into many classic political performances (see Edelman 1977, 1988). But behind the front-stage politics of the Reagan administration, there is a less obvious and probably more important dimension: the moral agenda of the New Right coalition that created the social and ideological foundation of the antidrug movement. In many ways, the mobilization of grass roots conservatism and get tough law and order ideologies that were manifest in the Reagan revolution combined to make a crackdown an almost inevitable expression of the feelings of this period.

As Joel Krieger has shown, a coalition of evangelical Christians, corporate sponsors, and traditional conservatives was largely responsible for the Reagan revolution. The former group, enjoying its newfound influence, took the forefront in attempting to set the moral agenda in the United States (Krieger 1986). From the "status politics" perspective developed by Gusfield (1963), social groups receive benefit from perceiving themselves as *the* model of good living in the society and, when threatened, defend their position as strongly as they might defend a more tangible benefit of the political order. Gusfield's recognition of the political stakes involved in the construction of public morality helps to make sense of a number of dynamics related to the rise of the New Right in American politics.

In this period, organizations like Toughlove began to grow (Trebach 1987, 65), and affiliated parents increasingly turned to strict discipline and incarceration for troublesome children. But the "toughlove" orientation would be extended beyond the children, because the agenda of the New Right was intended for the nation at large. The themes were family and traditional values, and soon there were seriously considered calls for school prayer, for the outlawing of offensive literature, for the censoring of rock lyrics, for the prohibition of abortion, for a restrengthening of the patriarchal family unit, and for other programs encouraging the right wing's vision of traditional morality.[15] Most of these bids required the expansion and intensification of the government's power over citizens' thoughts and actions. As Krieger summarized, the conservative policies of the Reagan coalition "represent sustained efforts not to 'get the state off our backs,' but to move the state into bedrooms, bath houses and school rooms—places where it had not previously been invited" (1986, 145).

Law and Order in the Reagan Years

The expansion of the punitive state was an almost unavoidable outgrowth of this period. At the core of the official ideology of the War on Drugs was the conservative movement's reassertion of a view of social problems and human behavior that centers on individual volition as the cause of crime and deterrence as the solution. Specifically rejecting a focus on the environmental or structural causes of human behavior, leading figures in the war espoused a theory of society and criminology in which autonomous individuals choose to deviate. Since causes of behavior are internal and rational, it follows that there is no need to focus on changing structural or environmental conditions that may be supporting social problems.[16] The response of the state should be to create a social context that forbids us from choosing to misbehave; people must believe that they will be caught and punished if they break the rules.

Take, for example, a telling exchange during the testimony of Dr. Robert DuPont, an antidrug professional since the Nixon administration and a private sector consultant on the implementation of drug-testing programs. In the winter of 1985 DuPont was speaking before the House Subcommittee on Safety and Health, which was holding Occupational Safety and Health Administration (OSHA) oversight hearings on drug use in the workplace.

> Too many people say that people use drugs for complex reasons. People identify perfectly sound psychological, social, economic problems, and then they hang them on drugs. People, it is said, use drugs, because they are poor, people use drugs because they are bored, people use drugs because they are angry, people use drugs because they are unhappy. Well the other side of this is equally true. People use drugs because they are rich. People use drugs because they are busy, people use drugs because they are happy, people use drugs because they are hot. . . .
> I ask the committee not to be too quick to buy into any explanation of why people are using drugs, however sophisticated it may sound, because I think you are likely to go astray. This thinking leads you to believe we have got to make work less boring, or less busy or whatever else to reduce drug use. That is the wrong conclusion. . . . You have to prevent drug use by saying no to using drugs. You cannot do it any other way. People do use drugs because they want to. People do it because they like it. What you have to do is establish a social environment that says no to the use of drugs for any and all reasons. (OSHA Oversight Hearings 1985, 18–19)

Although DuPont urges the committee to resist buying into any explanation of why people use drugs, he is, of course, offering his own explanation: people do things (use drugs, commit crimes) because they choose to.[17] As Walker observed,

> Individual responsibility reigns in the idealized conservative world. People who break rules should be punished. Punishment works, for an unpleasant sanction teaches a useful lesson. Criminals learn to obey the rules and others learn by their example that crime does not pay. (Walker 1989, 11)

To combat the drug problem authorities should, therefore, "establish a social environment that says no" with a dense system of surveillance and punishment. Stephen Schulhofer explains how drug-testing programs fit into this regime:

> Testing threatens millions of Americans with the speedy, inexpensive infliction of a sanction—unemployment—that has far more sting than the criminal penalties usually imposed for casual drug use. As a deterrent, employment testing can be extremely effective, regardless of its relation to on-the-job performance. (1989, 129)

This approach to law and order centers official attention on all the things pushed by the drug warriors—close observation, strict rules, and ongoing enforcement of personal and hierarchical discipline. The emergent remedy for social problems like drug use or crime is to create a network of control and punishment that is dense and severe enough to deter people from choosing to misbehave. The result was the crackdown manifest in such things as longer jail terms, more pervasive policing, and employee drug testing.

Conclusion

This chapter has discussed some of the many factors that came together to bring about the social construction of the crisis and crackdown surrounding illegal drug use in the mid-1980s. Mass media news coverage, political posturing, ideologically driven perception and policymaking, the appearance of crack cocaine, and ongoing patterns of illegal drug use all contributed to this remarkable cultural episode.

It should be clear that this exploration of the politics of the drug crisis has not argued that America was without some form of a "drug problem"—we clearly faced and face pressing but specific problems related to crack cocaine and the violence associated with wars over its distribution amid the poverty and hopelessness of the abandoned inner city. This situation is a tragedy calling for effective action that goes far beyond beatings and mass incarceration. But it is assuredly not a societywide national crisis of drug use that pervades families and workplaces across America.

In the context of this book, the political dynamics of the drug crisis and ensuing war on drugs are given this all-too-brief sketch because of their importance in understanding the broad popular context in which testing emerged. Turning back to the language and framework of ideological hegemony discussed in chapter 1, this crisis, much like the one studied by Hall and his colleagues (1978), generated a public mood that was ready to support innovative and dramatic actions promoted by elite policy entrepreneurs.[18]

In another time and place, those innovative and dramatic actions to fight drug use might have taken the form of a revolution in public education or a serious effort to deal with inequality and poverty in America. But the conservative law and order philosophy that prevailed in the 1980s eschewed such strategies as ineffective and turned instead to heightened surveillance and tougher punishments. Testing was a central tool in the arsenal; the next chapter explores this policy in detail and develops a theoretical framework for understanding its origins and significance.

Chapter 3

The Testers: Safety, Productivity, and the Surveillance Paradigm

Authoritative attempts to detect and limit illegal drug use have traditionally been carried out through the criminal law enforcement powers of the state. Employee drug testing expands on these efforts by deploying the apparatus of surveillance into the daily world of the workplace. While the state remains very active in traditional forms of drug control, it is also able to extend its reach into more diffuse and pervasive social contexts. As Reagan attorney general, Edwin Meese, put it, "Since most Americans work, 'the workplace can be the chokepoint' for halting drug abuse" (*New York Times*, October 31, 1986, 17). Drug testing, in this sense, is part of a broader change in social control policy that has been called a "widening of the net and thinning of the mesh": the net of control covers a larger area of the social ocean and is able to catch more and smaller fish—that is, those who break the rules (Cohen 1985, 42–43).[1]

Drug testing is anything but an isolated policy. Rather, it is one part of a widespread shift in control policy that is taking place in many sectors of the society: the workplace, welfare programs, schools, and other less formal settings in which new means of systematic surveillance are enhancing authorities' ability to monitor behavior. These new means include such things as computer matching for welfare fraud and income tax evasion (Reichman 1987), drunk driver checkpoints (Jacobs 1988), the computerization of police records (Rule 1973), eavesdropping on international phone calls (Marx 1986), and other recent innovations in surveillance techniques (see generally Marx 1986; Rule et al. 1980).[2]

To explain drug testing as both a part of this broader movement and as a phenomenon specifically rooted in the context of the contemporary workplace, this chapter explores two distinct bodies of literature. We begin in the workplace, with an attempt to sort out the multiple claims and interests surrounding the politics of workplace safety, productivity, and control. There are many reasons why different employers implemented employee drug testing. Some were virtually forced to by insurance companies or government regulations. Others wanted to support President Reagan's War on Drugs (Schulhofer 1989, 128). Clearly, much of the momentum was driven by the aggressive marketing of this cheap new technological means of workplace surveillance (Zimmer and Jacobs 1992).

More than one analysis of the rise of drug testing has included an element of technological determinism in explaining its sudden emergence (Walsh and Trumble 1991; Zimmer and Jacobs 1992). From this perspective, the emergence of an innovative technique for inexpensively testing large populations not only made testing programs possible but helped to create the very sense that testing was needed. In this light, it is worth noting that employers who had largely ignored casual off-duty drug use in the 1970s turned to it as a major problem once low-cost immunoassay techniques were available. But while technological development is an important part of understanding testing and other recent changes in high-technology surveillance policy (Marx and Reichman 1984), techniques do not market and implement themselves. Clearly the rapid and dramatic expansion of workplace testing policies must be framed within the struggles and concerns of the contemporary workplace.

The most fundamental and widely heard reasons for the promotion of testing programs were improving workplace safety and increasing employee productivity. But a critical assessment of the claims surrounding drug testing reveals a series of anomalies in arguments linking these programs to a straightforward interest in improving the health and safety of workers. The discussion will be decidedly atheoretical for a time while it is shown that most drug-testing programs have less to do with safety than might seem apparent; indeed, some analysts argue that they may even be counterproductive since they misidentify problems, alienate workers, and deplete resources from other policies. Another oddity that emerges in this policy story is that the main proponents of drug testing—corporate employers and the Reagan administration—have been among the greatest foes of a wide range of policies seeking to improve health and safety in the American workplace.

These anomalies in the rationale behind testing cue us to look for other ways to explain and understand the emergence of the policies. Here, an understanding of the politics of control in the workplace provides a framework that offers both a compelling explanation for why drug-testing policies are so strongly pursued and a critical account of who wins and who loses in the face of such policy initiatives.

But testing must also be placed in the broader context of fundamental changes in the organization of control. There appears to be, as Foucault (1979) put it, a "disciplining" of our society marked by the increasing use of surveillance techniques in an ever more universal and pervasive effort to establish and enforce norms. By turning to this more comprehensive analysis of changes in the means of control, we are able to establish a wider historical framework for assessing the issues studied here. We will also see that the broad poststructuralist account and the more specific analysis of workplace politics arrive at virtually identical conclusions about the contemporary nature of workplace control as well as the ongoing struggles over its constitution.

The Political Economy of Workplace Control

The Politics of Safety

They should do it in the interest of safety . . . . As a result of drug testing in American industry, the number of job related accidents is beginning to go down.

—Peter Bensinger

Everyone supports workplace safety. Trade unionists speak of safety as they educate their members about safe practices and try to pass laws to prevent employers from pursuing dangerous policies. Neoconservatives speak of safety and argue that regulation is the wrong road to safety—not that safety is bad but that safety comes along with the wealth derived from unregulated development and profit (Wildavsky 1980). Employers speak of safety and often argue that most accidents are caused by employees. The Reagan administration spoke of safety at the same time that it drastically limited OSHA's regulation and inspection of workplaces (Ferguson and Rogers 1986, 130–31; McCann 1986, 236).

Support for safety appears to rank with support for motherhood and opposition to illegal drugs as a valence symbol in politics. But there is more than one road to safety. Different roads to safety imply different and often competing values and are supported by different and competing economic and political interests. As will be explained, the trade unionists and public interest activists of the 1960s and 1970s argued that the most significant threats to workplace safety come from the workplace environment. Neoconservatives and their allies in the business world echo the law and order philosophy discussed earlier and argue that the most significant threats to safety come from the error or malfeasance of individual workers. As will be explained below, there are important ramifications in the ascendance of this latter perspective as manifest in the employee drug-testing movement.

Testing and Safety

This section began with a characteristic quote from Peter Bensinger, the former DEA director who is now with DuPont, Bensinger and Associates, a politically active private sector supporter of testing and provider of industrial drug-testing consulting services. Bensinger's comment highlights the fact that one of the most strongly perceived and oft-cited reasons for supporting drug testing is that it can improve workplace safety. Both government and private sector documents covering the implementation of drug testing cite workplace safety as the central reason for testing. The rub is that research by Charles Noble (1986), John Morgan (1988), and others (Guerrero 1987) shows that no one is all that sure about how many accidents are caused by drug use or about which policies actually do serve to reduce accident levels.

Bensinger, however, argues that the results are clear. He was hired by Georgia Power to implement drug testing at the construction site of a new nuclear power plant. He used surprise random testing, hotlines through which workers could be turned in, and highly invasive testing procedures (Weiss 1986). In his evaluation of the program, Bensinger wrote,

We note in our report that lost time accident rates have decreased from 5.41 accidents per 200,000 manhours in 1981 to less than 0.5 accidents in 1985. This remarkable achievement may not necessarily be attributed to the anti-drug program, but increased supervisory attention, drug-policy job-site awareness, extensive drug testing, and management commitment to the anti-drug program have probably been significant contributing factors. (Guerrero 1987, 23)

Bensinger's report provided statistical figures that seemed to support his conclusions about the necessity and efficacy of testing. The following numbers show the year followed by the number of accidents per 200,000 work hours at the job site (Guerrero 1987).

Year	Accident rate
1981	5.41
1982	2.09
1983	0.91
1984	0.61
1985	0.49

This is certainly an excellent rate of improvement. Were it clear that the drug-testing program made an important contribution to the changes, then we might not only be able to say that drug testing was an effective response but, by implication, that many workplace accidents prior to the testing program were attributable to employee drug use. But Guerrero's findings suggest otherwise:

Indeed, 5.41 down to less than 0.5. However the report does not, in listing the data, point out when drug testing actually began at Plant Vogtle—in April/May 1984. In fact as you can see, drug testing played a negligible role, if any, in improving safety. (Guerrero 1987, 23)

Thus, Bensinger's "success" in Georgia—which was prominently treated in both the legal and popular press[3]—was little more than sleight of hand. But what accounted for the decline in the accident rate? Guerrero credits a safety first campaign, but other analysts might be more likely to note the establishment of routine procedures and a familiar workforce after the first year at the construction site, the changing nature of work as construction proceeded, or other environmental factors. In this case, at least, drugs were apparently not a major cause of the problem and the drug-testing program was not a significant part of the cure.

But what about widely circulated figures showing that workplace drug use was racking up huge costs in the 1980s? One of the most prominent sets of figures cited in protesting arguments comes from the Firestone Study. Testing advocates who rely on the Firestone Study present a number of striking conclusions that would seem to compel employers to test: drug users are almost 4 times as likely to be involved in plant accidents, 2.5 times as likely to be absent for more than a week, and 5 times as likely to file workers' compensation claims, and they receive 3 times the average level of such benefits.

These figures originated from an in-house study done through the Employee Assistance Program (EAP) at the Firestone Tire and Rubber Company (Morgan 1988, 683–85). While skeptical researchers have never been allowed to see the original data, it has been learned that the figures "refer only to alcoholics who have been served by Firestone EAP" (Morgan 1988, 685). This study was therefore based solely on an analysis of individuals who had been sufficiently impaired by alcohol to either volunteer for or be ordered into the professional counseling program. The extrapolation to all working Americans who use illegal drugs—as the Partnership for a Drug Free America and the U.S. Chamber of Commerce did—is entirely inappropriate. "The statistics generated . . . have nothing to do with drug users, recreational or otherwise" (Morgan 1988, 685). Nonetheless, these figures are widely and repeatedly cited, creating a pseudoscientific impression of firm knowledge about the impact of drugs in the workplace.

By the late 1980s, drug-testing programs were having the ironic effect of showing that most workplaces probably didn't need drug-testing programs. While there are obviously dangerously intoxicated people in some workplaces, studies like those reviewed below have begun to show that early claims about the extent and impact of drug use were wildly exaggerated.

In January 1987, a tragic railroad accident involving an engineer and an assistant who had smoked marijuana on the job resulted in the loss of sixteen lives. Headlines and congressional hearings emphasized the hypothesized link between the drug and the accident, and the incident was a clear impetus for the drug-testing movement as a whole. But what went unmentioned were the results of an eleven-month drug-testing program in the rail industry. This Federal Rail Administration (FRA) program of postaccident testing encompassed some 175 accidents and led to the testing of 759 employees. Of those 759, there were 43 positive results, including 9 for alcohol,[4] 29 for illicit substances, and 14 for other controlled substances. Of the 29 for illicit substances, 18 tested positive for the marijuana metabolite, 5 were positive for a cocaine metabolite, and 6 were positive for both (Morgan 1988, 691, citing the FRA report).

The results of this testing program fail to show a convincing and general link between accidents and drug use. The percentage of personnel that tested positive (3.8) simply did not indicate a significant causal role in the accidents and was, in fact, less than that found in some other testing programs. As the FRA concluded, the "data are not conclusive of [sic] alcohol/drug role in industrial accidents" (quoted in Morgan 1988, 692).[5] Indeed, seven of the twenty-nine workers who tested positive for illegal drug use worked on jobs "which would seem to place them at a distance from operating decisions (track patroller, ticket taker, conductor, road master)" (Morgan 1988, 692). Results such as these led the FRA to conclude in 1988 that levels of drug use in the railroad industry were "below many previous estimates."[6]

What appears to be the best available study on these issues was published in the November 1990 issue of the *Journal of the American Medical Association*. Zwerling, Ryan, and Orav (1990) conducted prehire testing of 2,537 post office job applicants and then tracked their performance for an average of 406 calendar days. During this period, they found that those testing positive for having used marijuana at some point in the month preceding their employment had a slightly elevated risk of accidents: 1.55 with a 95 percent confidence interval. In plainer language, those testing positive for marijuana use were somewhere between 1.16 and 2.08 times more likely to have an accident. The unadjusted figures on accident rates among these new postal workers showed that 19.2 percent of those who tested negative for drug use were involved in an accident, while 26.3 percent and 27.3 percent of those testing positive for, respectively, marijuana and cocaine were involved in accidents. The authors conclude that "[t]he findings of this study suggest that many of the claims cited to justify preemployment drug screening have been exaggerated" (Zwerling, Ryan, and Orav 1990).

Despite the careful analytical work of this study, it still leaves a good deal of uncertainty about the impact of drug use because the authors were unable to control for alcohol use, which is more widespread and believed to be more tightly linked to workplace accidents. Since individuals who use illegal drugs often use alcohol as well, the impact of the two factors undoubtedly runs together in many of these cases. Nonetheless, the results seem to suggest, as would common sense, that some people who use illegal drugs are more likely to have trouble in the workplace. There is little support, however, for the exaggerated claims of workplace crises and danger that accompanied the testing movement.

In promoting their testing initiative, Reagan administration officials were fond of claiming that at least a fifth of American workers were on drugs, but no reputable study has shown use rates anywhere near these claims. A 1988 study sponsored by the Labor Department in an effort to gauge the extent of drug testing and EAPs offers more data on the extent of drug use within certain industries and firms (U.S. Department of Labor 1989). These data relate only to certain industries and to the minority of firms that already had a drug-testing program in place[7] and responded to the researchers' queries. Most— around 80 percent—of the employees tested were tested *only after they had been suspected of drug use.* Even with this extensive preselection, only 8.8 percent showed positive tests for some type of illicit drug use sometime prior to the test.

More tellingly, a program that included randomized drug testing of more than 30,000 federal government employees has shown far lower levels of positive results (*Seattle Times*, March 8, 1989, A1, A5). In that random testing has no element of preselection, it is the best measure of actual rates of use within workplace populations. Ironically, the program clearly refuted the views of those who portray a workplace that is awash in illegal drugs by establishing a positive rate of 0.7 percent.[8] The article goes on to point out that the "overwhelming majority of those testing positive used marijuana, which can be detected in the urine as long as two months after it was smoked." It continued,

When job applicants and employees who acted suspiciously are included with workers caught up in random tests, the total tested so far is at least 49,751, with the results revealing a drug-use rate of 0.6 percent among reporting agencies.

Although we cannot know for sure, these figures may reflect a decline in drug use created by the deterrent effect of the drug tests themselves. But when we take these very low figures together with the critical assessment of impact studies presented earlier, it seems clear that there has been a good deal of exaggeration and misperception in the assessment of drug use and its impact on the American workplace.[9]

Of course, that is not to suggest that there are *no* impaired workers. That would be foolish. It is rather to suggest that policy formation, public debate, and legal decision making are taking place under the influence of poorly derived and grossly inflated premises about the extent of the problem (see also Hall et al. 1978).

The Context for Testing: Safety, Productivity, and Control

Business people are usually pretty smart about spending money, and they have been at the forefront of efforts to resist government policies intended to make them spend it on improving workplace health and safety. Why, then, was testing so enthusiastically pursued when it was not at all clear that it was sound investment? No single explanation can ever account for the behavior of many different individuals and firms—they face different situations, have different priorities and goals, and make different assessments of their options. Some employers undoubtedly faced particularly abusive workplaces, some were fooled by political claims and drug test sales representatives, some were coerced by insurance companies or government policy, some surely saw it as an act of patriotic support for President Reagan's War on Drugs.

Whatever the particular spark that led an individual corporation to pursue testing, a more comprehensive understanding of the societywide momentum that the testing movement enjoyed must look to the broader context in which testing flourished. The remainder of this chapter attempts to place testing in this broader context by focusing on the relationship between drug testing and contemporary struggles over the pursuit of safety, productivity, and control in the workplace.

Ideologies of Safety

Debates over the causes of workplace accidents have been a central part of the ongoing struggle over safety and the regulation and deregulation of the workplace environment. In the pre-OSHA days of the late 1960s, when public interest groups and labor unions argued that workplace conditions were responsible for high rates of injury and accident, business leaders countered by blaming the workers (Noble 1986, 46–47, 83–84). Citing an influx of young workers and a breakdown of discipline, industrial interests maintained a pattern that we now see continued in the drug-testing movement: shift the focus of the safety debate away from job conditions, work schedules, machinery design, productivity rates, and other factors controlled by the employer toward a questioning of the skill and integrity of the individual worker. With the worker defined as the problem, greater surveillance and control become the answer, and the balance of workplace power continues to accrue in the hands of management. Furthermore, with accidents perceived as the result of individual error or malfeasance, employers don't need to spend a lot of money working on solutions that call for changing the workplace environment or lowering the pace of production.

    Note, for example, the conflicting possible responses to prevent a recurrence of something like the Exxon *Valdez* oil spill. In the wake of the crisis, Exxon and the Coast Guard both responded in the vein established by corporations and conservative political administrations by stepping up the drug testing of employees. Yet a potentially more effective approach would be the double-hulled tanker long sought by environmentalists but strongly opposed by the oil companies and the allegedly proenvironment Bush administration. Indeed, Bush's secretary of transportation, Samuel Skinner—a backer of widespread employee drug testing (*Seattle Times*, December 18, 1989, A9)—was a point man in the administration's efforts to block a congressional bill requiring double hulls on oil tankers (*Seattle Times*, March 2, 1990, C2). The double hull bill represents a loss of corporate autonomy, a cost to corporate ledger sheets, and the implicit recognition that management behavior (opting for single hulls) is an important part of industrial accidents. Drug testing, on the other hand, costs far less, increases management power, and carries forward the focus on worker malfeasance as an explanation for industrial accidents.

This bid to shift the primary blame for workplace accidents away from management was clearly the ideological and economic victor in the 1980s. The Reagan administration is widely noted for its lax approach to enforcing workplace safety standards. As Noble concludes after evaluating OSHA rule making and rates of inspection and enforcement in the 1980s,

> The basic pattern signaled by Reagan in 1980 and endorsed by [OSHA-head Thorne] Auchter held. As an enforcement agency, OSHA was rendered toothless. It became, instead, an advocate for the employer's point of view on occupational hazards. (1986, 196)[10]

The "employer's point of view" tends to hold that safety, in the words of the American Iron and Steel Institute, "would require far more consideration of the man rather than the environment" (quoted in Noble 1986, 84). In this way, the emergent ideology of safety is identical to the volitional ideology of crime and drug use put forth by the Reagan administration officials and conservative academics seen in the preceding chapter. These frameworks identify social phenomena as originating with individual choices rather than conditions in the environment or social structure. The implications of this way of thinking include less attention to changing the structural environments in which people live and more attention to establishing rewards, punishments, and systems of surveillance to deter people from misbehaving.

Consideration of the individual rather than the environment allows a greater proportion of capital to be devoted to business interests other than safety—such as profit. Not surprisingly, therefore, as Reagan was backing off on the enforcement of OSHA regulations, industry backed off on the amount of money spent on employee health and safety. While the years from 1972 to 1978 saw between 2 percent and 3 percent of capital investment going to worker health and safety, the figures dropped to between 1.4 percent and 1.6 percent from 1979 to the mid-1980s. The overall average from 1972 to 1983 was only 2.1 percent—nothing to boast about—but the downswing is noteworthy. Tellingly, then, the preface to all of the management rhetoric about workplace safety in the 1980s was initially low and then lower rates of investment in health and safety programs.

Above, we've seen that the "blame the worker" ideology associated with an approach like drug testing fits a pattern that deemphasizes regulation and shifts of corporate capital away from health and safety expenditures. But there is another, more subtle way in which such an ideology and policy may work in favor of management and against the struggle for a safe workplace. Evidence presented by Noble (1986) suggests that empowered employees who have the authority to truly participate in all key aspects of workplace management may be the best long-term solution to the safety problem.[11] If that is the case, then top-down disciplinary policies that bypass and displace worker control may actually work against safety.

Drug-testing programs have challenged and in some cases displaced alternative programs that were able to deal with drug use and other problems in ways that did not so directly degrade and exclude workers. Through Operation Stop, rail workers voiced their own opposition to workplace intoxication by setting up worker committees that provided referral services as well as a means of policing the ranks. Those involved report not just declining drug use but increasing morale as union members assert their own control over the work environment (see Wisman 1990). Health care professionals who run EAPs have voiced concern about testing programs because of fears that they will misdirect priorities away from alcohol abuse, mental health, and other problems and because testing programs might undermine the work of EAPs by creating an atmosphere of distrust (Bureau of National Affairs 1987; Denenburg and Denenburg 1987, 385).[12]

Noble's comparative analysis suggests that safety programs that empower workers rather than exclude them—such as those in some Western European countries (1986, 225–36) and in the rail industry's Operation Stop—more strongly serve safety interests because monitoring is in the hands of the workers rather than a vulnerable and politicized government bureau. Further, the involvement of workers strengthens their organizations and enhances their ability to make significant demands for improvements in the workplace environment. OSHA failed, in part, because it did almost the opposite. It entered the workplace as an outside force and, rather than enabling workers to take care of themselves, cast them as a dependent population in need of paternal assistance (Noble 1986, 67, 202–6). In this sense, although their focuses are quite different, drug-testing programs and other hierarchical policies may have been cut from the same cloth.

What we see in this account is that drug testing fits into a broader approach to workplace management and control that has marked the period from which testing emerged. First, the problems of the workplace are blamed on the malfeasance of workers, just as crime, poverty, and other social problems are blamed on the failures of individual citizens. Second, a hierarchically administered cure that places the entire work force under increased suspicion, surveillance, and control is prescribed. Programs that might empower workers and their unions, such as union-based EAPs, stronger education programs, or peer counseling, have been bypassed or even displaced (see Bookspan 1988, 397–98; Denenburg and Denenburg 1987, 384–85). The result is a work force that is defined as evil and troublesome, is administered a cure that enhances the power of both the state and their employers, and is further excluded from activities that might support empowerment and organization.

The Politics of Productivity

Management explanations for employee drug testing have at least as much to say about productivity as they do about safety. Productivity is the gold standard of the workplace, and drugs and drug testing have been closely associated with perceptions of a productivity problem and its solution. Indeed, testing consultant and proponent Peter Bensinger has gone so far as to blame employee drug use for the overall weakening of U.S. industrial performance in the late 1970s (Wisotsky 1987b, 767).

In this section, I discuss the politics of productivity in the workplace and the relationship of productivity levels to drug testing. I agree with other researchers who argue that drug testing has little to do with specific levels of productivity. Testing does, however, have a lot to do with broader tendencies in workplace control that are related to long-run productivity and profit. In the light of recent

research and theory on social control in the workplace, drug testing
fits well within the logic of an emergent system of bureaucratic control that is amending or displacing more traditional systems of
workplace supervision (Edwards 1979).

The Struggle for Control

The struggle over control of the workplace is, as Richard Edwards
explains in *Contested Terrain,* as old as capitalism itself. When the
employer hires the worker for a day's work, the conflict between
capital and labor has only begun. The employer must still struggle
to get as much actual labor out of the worker as he or she possibly
can. "He has purchased a given quantity of labor power, but he must
now . . . strive to extract actual labor from the labor power he legally
owns" (Edwards 1979, 12; see the discussion in Braverman 1974,
60–69).

> These basic relationships in production reveal both the basis
> for conflict and the problem of control at the workplace. . . .
> Conflict arises over how work shall be organized, what work
> pace shall be established, what conditions producers must labor
> under, what rights workers shall enjoy, and how the various
> employees of the enterprise shall relate to each other. The
> workplace becomes a battleground, as employers attempt to ex-
> tract the maximum effort from workers and workers necessarily
> resist their bosses' impositions. (Edwards 1979, 12, 13)

In the light of the employers' fundamental interest in increasing
levels of productivity and perceptions that drug use is lowering them,
it is not at all surprising that employers increasingly turn to drug
testing to monitor and correct the perceived situation. As a number
of researchers have pointed out, however, there is not a solid link
between the productivity interest and the drug-testing technology.
As Elinor Schroeder puts it,

> Presumably, current employees who test positive on a random
> or blanket drug screen have been performing at a satisfactory
> level; otherwise, the employer would already have disciplined
> or fired them. . . . More than one management lawyer has re-

ceived a call from a client asking, "Our best worker has just
tested positive. Do we have to fire him?" (1988, 874)

At a basic level, Schroeder is correct—drug tests measure neither present nor future productivity (see also Bookspan 1988; Morgan 1988; Wisotsky 1987b). Workers who are not producing at desired rates or who are obviously impaired in the workplace can be
detected and dealt with through traditional means of supervision.
Why then the costly and controversial move to drug testing? Arguments that drug tests are not reasonably related to productivity concerns—though accurate and important—presume too simplistic an
approach to social control in the workplace. Under contemporary
systems of workplace discipline, the relationship between management policies and productivity is more abstract than it used to be.
And in light of these new systems, drug testing is more plausibly
explained.

Historical changes in the organization of production have
brought changes in the organization of workplace control. In his
analysis, Edwards (1979) identifies three basic modes of control in the
workplace. The first, "personal control," is typified by individual
owners or bosses who are present on the shop floor and who distrib-
ute rewards and punishments for behavior that they either desire or
disdain.

But in large part, the days of small entrepreneurial shops are
over, and control can no longer be administered by an individual
keeping an eye on the workers. The shop floor has grown too big and
management too distant from it to rely on personal systems of control
(Burawoy 1979, 176; Edwards 1979, 27–30). Rather, contemporary
modes of workplace control increasingly rely on the use of more
sophisticated and efficient techniques to control employees.

Emerging in the twentieth century, the second mode, "technical
control," is a system of workplace organization based on designing
the actual structure of the factory to force optimal levels of output.
Thus, under Taylorism and other approaches to maximizing efficiency, machines set the pace of the work and the workers follow the
machines. The famous assembly line of the auto manufacturers is
probably the best expression of this system. In short, the problem of
controlling the rate of production is met by subordinating the worker
to the pace of the machine.

But the drive for the perfect worker as opposed to just the perfect rate of production is the key element in Edwards's third type of control: "bureaucratic control." Although bureaucratic control is a complex and multifaceted pattern of workplace organization that will always overlap with other forms of control, at its heart there is a fairly simple proposition: transcend the natural conflicts and difficulties of the "contested terrain" of the workplace by selecting and training workers who offer or can be taught to offer "no contest." Under bureaucratic control the traditional goals of increasing productivity and profit are pursued, in part, by shaping a work force that meets management's standards on criteria other than simple productivity.

Edwards explains this aspect of bureaucratic control:

> It is the indirect path to the intensification of work, through the mechanism of rewarding behavior relevant to the control system, rather than simply work itself, that imposes the new behavior requirements on workers.... Employers seek out and reward workers with the right behavior traits. (Edwards 1979, 148–49)

This orientation is readily apparent in a selection from Frederick Winslow Taylor's *The Principles of Scientific Management*. Here the father of scientific personnel management is explaining his successful efforts to nearly quadruple the amount of pig iron moved by laborers at Bethlehem Steel.

> Our first step was the scientific selection of the workman.... A careful study was ... made of each of these men. We looked up their history as far back as practicable and thorough inquiries were made as to the character, habits, and the ambitions of each of them. (quoted in Braverman 1974, 103)

As Schroeder notes in an article subtitled "Employer Monitoring and the Quest for the Perfect Worker,"

> It is only natural that employers will implement selection and supervision devices that hold out some promise, however slim,

of reducing costs and improving productivity. Thus, various selection devices that purport to identify workers who may be
costly to a firm for one reason or another, such as polygraph
examinations, drug tests, AIDS tests, and other forms of medical
and genetic screening, are in common use by many employers. . . . The ultimate goal of all employment selection, control,
and monitoring techniques is to find the "right" person for each
job and to obtain the maximum level of efficient production from
him or her, all at the lowest possible cost to the employer. (1988,
870, 873)

Thus, while drug tests cannot measure actual rates of productivity, they may be able to assist in the selection or creation of what
management perceives to be "the perfect worker."

From the perspective of Edwards's analysis, managers who assert that drug testing will increase productivity, or critics who point
out that drug testing measures neither productivity nor impairment,
sidestep or overlook an essential point. The premise that management concerns are limited to actual rates of productivity or simple
ability to function is outmoded. The contemporary approach to increasing discipline and productivity is a far more encompassing strategy that seeks to find (or make) "the good worker" (Edwards 1979,
147). And the "good worker" is defined as not only one who meets
productivity demands but one who adapts well to the system of
bureaucratic control. Edwards points out that for jobs below the management level, the most strongly desired characteristic of the good
worker is "rules orientation"—"an awareness of rules and a sustained propensity to follow them" (1979, 149). While drug tests may
not measure productivity or impairment, they can measure this characteristic, since one who uses illegal drugs is by definition a violator
of official rules.

The implications of this new system are not overlooked by Edwards, who argues,

There existed a certain breathing space inside prebureaucratic
control. . . . Bureaucratic control tends to be a much more totalitarian system—totalitarian in the sense of including the total
behavior of the worker. (1979, 147–48)

The Surveillance Paradigm

The preceding pages have focused solely on the workplace and the particular combination of issues and incentives related to the testing movement in that specific context. But testing, as suggested earlier, is part of a broader movement in social control that centers on the general intensification of surveillance throughout the society. In the 1980 collection entitled *Power/Knowledge*, Michel Foucault describes the possibilities inherent in the power of "the gaze":

> There is no need for arms, physical violence, material con-straints. Just a gaze. An inspecting gaze, a gaze which each individual under its weight will end by interiorising to the point that he is his own overseer, each individual thus exercising this surveillance over, and against, himself. A superb formula: power exercised continuously and for what turns out to be a minimal cost. (Foucault 1980b, 155)

There are obvious and important connections between a devel-opment like employee drug testing and the broader patterns of social change described by Foucault. Not surprisingly, aspects of his work are being productively applied to analyses of social control (Cohen 1985), criminological surveillance, and, more specifically, employee drug testing (Hanson 1988). As Cohen put it, perhaps overstating things a bit, "To write today about punishment and classification without Foucault, is like talking about the unconscious without Freud" (1985, 10).

Systems of Control

Many of those who apply Foucault's insights to issues of surveillance and criminology center on his *Discipline and Punish*.[13] Although that work is explicitly a study of the "birth of the prison," in it Foucault traces the emergence of the broader "disciplinary society"—a world in which surveillance is nearly constant, in which the control sciences of medicine and administration are worked out to their finest detail, and in which the visible power of the king is replaced by the invisible power of "the disciplines."[14]

According to Foucault, the disciplinary system of power has emerged as an alternative to the "juridical system" sought by Enlightenment reformers and expressed in many aspects of our legal system. The juridical system lies at the heart of liberal analyses of politics— the limited state, the social contract, and a vision of political power as something that is held or unleashed at the will of the powerful. It is, importantly, a system based on a matrix of rights, entitlements, and duties; obedience was owed to the state, and those who disobeyed and were caught were punished as violators of a social contract and according to the stipulations of the legal code.[15]

The carefully administered punishments of the juridical system had replaced the horrendous tortures of the previous period in which crimes were seen as an affront to the monarch and were met with an intense unleashing of power. While the juridical system thus represented a significant change in the mode and standards of punishment, in one way it continued the practices of antiquity. That is, the administration of social control within both of these earlier systems manifested a "crime and (then) punishment" approach to law and order: the authorities *reacted* to misbehavior. Individuals who were detected in violations of the law were severely and publicly punished (classic) or moderately and publicly punished (juridical). Whatever the organization of punishment, though, the organization of surveillance and apprehension was a more haphazard and partial matter.

Under disciplinary power, control no longer emanates from the throne, and contracts, rights, and duties no longer express the organization of power. Rather, power works as an endlessly diffuse and circulating force that does less to deny than it does to shape and create. This change is vividly manifest in the emergent system of social control. Previously, the power of control was wielded when representatives of the state caught someone violating the law and then used their power to punish that individual. Under the disciplinary system, surveillance and control is more constant and diffuse and less punitive. As Stanley Cohen describes it,

> [T]he subject was to be observed, retrained and rendered obedient, not just punished along some abstract scale of justice. And the prison, instead of being just one landmark in the punitive city, now came to monopolize and symbolize all forms of punishment. Surveillance and not just punishment became the object of the exercise. . . . "[p]anopticism" emerged as a new modality of control throughout society. (1985, 26)

Panopticism

Panopticism is essential in the disciplinary society; surveillance must be made both constant and ubiquitous (see Dreyfus and Rabinow 1983, 156–59). Each individual becomes the object of careful and intricate examination and judgment such that each small violation of the norms can be detected and dealt with. Over time, the subject-citizens are slowly trained to discipline themselves—the mentality of the watcher or supervisor becomes internalized and is so manifestly present that, as Jeremy Bentham hoped, the very thought of deviance becomes more difficult to entertain.

> It is obvious that, in all these instances, the more constantly the persons to be inspected are under the eyes of the persons who should inspect them, the more perfectly will the purpose of the establishment have been attained. Ideal perfection, if that were the object, would require that each person should actually be in that predicament during every instant of time. (Bentham 1962, 40)

Bentham "recommended the panopticon as an ideal arrangement for any large institution: insane asylums, hospitals, orphanages, schools and factories . . . " (Hanson 1988, 912; see also Bentham 1962; Foucault 1979, 211). The panopticon is a cylindrical building in which the cells make up the walls of the cylinder. In the center is a tower from which an observer can look into any of the cells at any time without the inhabitant knowing that surveillance is occurring. While it may not seem apparent to the modern eye, the simple notion of individual cells is of great significance in the panoptic complex. In the teeming dungeons and chambers of earlier penitentiaries, detailed knowledge was impossible—the body of prisoners was a mass, behaviors could go unnoticed, punishment was a hit-and-miss post hoc affair.

In the panopticon, however, no one can hide, information is microscopic and specific, and the mentality of the mass is broken. The constantly observed subject is rewarded for normal behavior and punished or counseled for deviance. In this way, the subject is conditioned. In time, the prisoner who lives under this constant and unverifiable observation becomes a subjectivity that is grounded in existence as an object of observation. The subject "internalizes the gaze," and the good behavior that results manifests what can be called "self-

discipline," but it is the discipline of a "self" constituted by the ongoing enforcement of norms (see also Hanson 1988, 912–13; Poster 1984,
100–102).

Since detailed and total information is essential to the disciplinary society, one can easily see how a biological examination such as
a drug test would fit into the machinery of administration.[16] The
ability of drug tests to provide thorough and comprehensive information on misbehavior undertaken at any moment and location marks
them as a panoptic device that is free from the limits of space and
time. The tests' power to pull the individual out of the mass and lay
him or her open for a scientific survey of behavior around-the-clock
clearly replicates the forms of observation implemented in the panopticon. The inability of the individual to predict when tests occur and
the anonymity of the medical technician who administers the test also
express fundamental criteria of disciplinary techniques.

Surveillance as Power

It is a basic premise of the Enlightenment period that a controlled
gathering of information is the first step in taking reasoned action.
In this sense, an observation process like drug testing is consonant
with one of the central themes in contemporary Western culture: as
rationalists, we gather information and then we act. Foucault, however, argues that the investigation itself is a mechanism of power. In
his view, the examination—whether scholastic, psychological, or
medical—is part of the disciplining process that marks the nature of
power in contemporary society.

> The investigation was an authoritarian search for truth observed
> or attested and was thus opposed to the old procedures of the
> oath, the ordeal, the judicial dual, the judgement of God or even
> to the transaction between private individuals. The investigation
> was the sovereign power arrogating to itself the right to establish
> the truth by a number of regulated techniques. (Foucault 1979, 225)

In every area of modern life, an inspection of the subject—the
fact-finding trip, the surgeon general's report, the midterm examination, the drug test, the criminal trial—is essential to legitimate
authoritative action. The crucial insight in Foucault's work, however,

is to revise our perception of the relation of knowledge and power. Traditional liberal conceptualizations frame knowledge as being separate from and antecedent to the exercise of power. But Foucault rejects the question of legitimacy and unites power and knowledge, recognizing that structures of power in the society shape structures of knowledge, and vice versa, and that surveillance itself is a mode of power.

> The exercise of discipline presupposes a mechanism that coerces by means of observation; an apparatus in which the techniques that make it possible to see induce effects of power, and in which, conversely, the means of coercion make those on whom they are applied clearly visible. (Foucault 1979, 170–71)

In this light, a surveillance program such as drug testing is not merely an exploratory antecedent to the activities of control—though it may well precede actions such as counseling, imprisonment, suspension, or job loss. Rather, it is a central aspect of the process of discipline itself. "Hence the central effect of the Panopticon: to induce in the inmate a state of conscious and permanent visibility that assures the automatic functioning of power" (Foucault 1979, 201; see also Poster 1984, 102). It enforces our visibility and our status as objects within the institution. Where in prior ages the kings and princes were visible and the commoners anonymous, "disciplinary power . . . imposes on those whom it subjects a principle of compulsory visibility. In discipline it is the subjects who have to be seen" (Foucault 1979, 187).[17]

This way of thinking about surveillance challenges us to change the way we think about a variety of surveillance and assessment policies. They do not merely assist or refine other more traditional mechanisms of power such as punishment and reward. Surveillance is itself a power mechanism that changes not just behavior but the very individual who is ceaselessly exposed to the gaze.

Conclusion: Discipline, Bureaucratic Control, and the Law

It has been argued that the interests and ideology of corporate managers create a number of incentives to pursue policies that indict and disempower workers through increased surveillance and control. As a bid to displace regulatory movements that center on controlling management rather than workers and as a policy that dramatically intensifies the scope and density of employer control, drug-testing programs advance a number of management interests. At a second and broader level of analysis, it has been shown that testing is one element of a longer historical reorientation in the organization of social control. Here, uniting the specific with the general, we see that the disciplinary society described by Foucault and the workplace control system explained by Edwards and others reviewed in this chapter are virtually one and the same. The emergent orientation to social control that both authors envision is marked by several important characteristics.

1. It centers on the use of disciplinary techniques to carefully monitor and work toward the elimination of deviance. Rather than waiting for deviance to occur, the energies of the program work toward eliminating the possibility of deviance itself. Through surveillance, long-term training, incentives against deviance, and the elimination of the recalcitrant, the problems that older methods of control responded to are increasingly precluded.

2. In working toward the elimination of deviance, the focus of control shifts away from specific productivity rates or other manifestations of obedience. Rather, the focus is on normal behavior itself. We see the shift away from the monitoring of production rates to the development of the "perfect worker." "The main concern seems to be not measuring output but instead checking compliance with the rules" (Edwards 1979, 140).

3. Additionally, as with any system of bureaucratization, personal authority grows less visible and important—"the impersonal force of 'company rules' or 'company policy' [is] the basis for control" (Edwards 1979, 131). In Foucault's analysis, the personage of the prince or king declines as the diffuse and multiple sites of discipline become the crucial regions of control.

4. Finally, the center of visibility shifts. While the shop owner or the prince was on display and visibly present in earlier

modes, in the disciplinary realm, the previously anonymous worker or subject becomes the center of surveillance and analysis. The commoner is surrounded by video and computer monitors, by drug tests, by DNA analysis, and by intricate record keeping of the individual's educational, employment, and financial history.

For the topic at hand, it is the use of ongoing surveillance in the effort to produce normal behavior on a continuous basis that is of greatest importance. The biological monitoring manifest in drug testing creates an around-the-clock system of observation that is far more exact, in-depth, and totalizing than human authorities could ever produce on their own. The worker may not be a worker from just seven o'clock to four o'clock, nor can the citizen just pay taxes and offer a salute on the occasional holiday. Disciplinary power "is a type of power which is constantly exercised by means of surveillance rather than in a discontinuous manner by means of a system of levies or obligations distributed over time" (Foucault 1980b, 104).

Just as both Foucauldian and neo-Marxian analyses reach similar conclusions about the emergent modes of control, they also reach similar conclusions about the likely nature of conflict over and opposition to the implementation of this control. In each framework, it is a legal rights claim that emerges as the most likely course of action.[18] In Edwards's analysis, the legal claim is the most likely vehicle of resistance because the implementation of bureaucratic control means that the "rule of law" enters the workplace. Regulations, contracts, and legal procedures become the means of control in the workplace, but (in the double-edged outcome that seems typical of any use of the law) workers can also use legal procedures to challenge changes in policy.

> For the particular questions of the organization of work, job conditions, and the rights of workers, bureaucratic control tended to hasten political intervention. Bureaucratic control's reliance on formal rules and procedures . . . on rule of corporate law in place of rule by command—invited political struggle to alter those rules. . . . More generally, workers turn to the state to amend, shape, and dictate the rules of bureaucratic control. (Edwards 1979, 161)

Edwards goes on to cite a multitude of legal actions and settlements in which workers have used the legal apparatus of the state to influence the political struggle within the workplace. By using the rule of law *in* the workplace, it seems, managers contributed to the application of the rule of law *to* the workplace. Thus, in the face of a policy change such as drug testing, we should expect legalistic claims to emerge as the expression of worker opposition.

Foucault makes an even stronger case for expecting resistance to take a legalistic form. The foundation of his argument lies in the coexistence of two antithetical systems of power in the contemporary order. One, of course, is "disciplinary power"—the diffuse circulating manifestation of domination throughout society. But the other is the older form that refused to die: juridical power. As discussed earlier, juridical power is the power of legal rights and obligations that was constructed around the thrones of kings.[19] The two systems of power are antithetical; while disciplinary power is concerned only with what is *effective* in producing normalized behavior, juridical power concerns itself with what is *legitimate*—when the state should be limited, when the citizen must obey.

> The discourse of discipline has nothing in common with that of law, rule, or sovereign will. . . . The code they come to define is not that of law but of normalization. . . . It is human science which constitutes their domain, and clinical knowledge their jurisprudence. (Foucault 1980b, 107)

It is from the conflict between these two orders of power that we draw the expectation that a grievance related to the disciplines may be expressed through recourse to the system of rights.

> Against the usurpations by the disciplinary mechanism, against this ascent of a power that is tied to scientific knowledge, we find that there is no solid recourse available to us today, such being our situation, except that which lies precisely in the return to a theory of right organized around sovereignty and articulated upon its ancient principle. When today one wants to object in some way to the discipline and all the effects of power and knowledge that are linked to them, what is it that one does . . . if

not precisely appeal to this canon of right, this famous formal
right . . . ? (Foucault 1980b, 107–8)[20]

As will be discussed in later chapters, a turn to rights may be far
from the best bet in the construction of effective resistance. But as
shown in chapter 4, it is clear where workers who oppose drug testing turn. They turn to "this famous formal right."

Chapter 4

The Tested: Consent and Resistance in the Unionized Work Force

"Now a high paid man does just what he's told to do, and no back talk. Do you understand that?"
— Frederick Winslow Taylor

I strongly oppose drug testing because it invades my privacy. . . . I will not sell out my constitutional rights for a couple bucks an hour raise in wages.
— a craftsman

In 1988, I was interviewing a union official on the issues surrounding the drug-testing controversy. He was a representative for a labor union local with a membership of roughly 5,000 skilled workers.[1] The craft performed by the membership is needed in workplaces as varied as construction sites, transportation services, public utilities, and large-scale manufacturing. The nature of the work puts safety and technical excellence at the forefront of concerns. In the context of the late 1980s, the safety concern meant that drug testing was in the offing for much of the union's membership.

Having learned this, I asked the official a question asked of every other union official I had interviewed: "How does your membership feel about drug testing?" Others had typically said things like, "They support it," "They oppose it," or "They only care about wages, vacations, and benefits." But this time, I got a different answer: "I don't have the slightest idea."

This was probably the honest answer for most employers, union officials, government bureaucrats, and other decision makers in the drug-testing controversy. As drugs and testing got their share of press attention in the late 1980s, Americans learned about the opinions and arguments of the Reagan administration, the ACLU, and a handful of employers and union representatives. But it was more difficult to learn about what workers themselves felt.

Since they are the ones who would have the best knowledge of the extent and impact of workplace drug use and the most personally authoritative views on whether or not testing violated their rights to privacy and due process and would, of course, be the ones actually subject to testing, it only makes sense to turn to workers as experts on testing. Fortuitously, my conversation with the union official opened the door to research that tried to get a handle on how workers saw the testing initiative.

By listening to how workers feel about testing, we can also learn a great deal about some of the broader questions of this project. We will see that workers' views on testing were significantly affected by the sense of a national drug crisis that prevailed in the late 1980s. This result would appear to affirm some of the arguments about ideological hegemony that were considered in chapter 1: the image of a national drug crisis *did* bring many workers to accept significant intrusions into their lives.

But other factors were even more important, such as workers' assessments of drug use in their own workplace and, more importantly, their beliefs about whether testing violated rights to privacy and due process. These results clearly challenge simple arguments about the relationship between crises and popular politics: crises can win acquiescence, but there are other contexts and values that can and will mitigate their impact.

Importantly, the chief mitigator seems to be the cultural abstraction known as a *right*. Legal rights claims are the centerpiece of workers' explanations of why they oppose testing. To most of us, that probably seems likely, even inevitable, in a society that appears to be dominated by lawyers and litigation. It is this very sense of the inevitability and almost universal centrality of legal discourse that must be closely examined. What are the implications of the turn to rights? What does it mean when millions of people express themselves with words like *rights, due process,* and *privacy*?

In some ways it suggests a people empowered by a sense of legal entitlement and enabled by a shared vocabulary of resistance. Rights can appear to be a discourse of entitlement that breaks the hegemonic grip of the drug warriors and comes alive as a vocabulary of resistance and collective action. But such a framing ignores the extent to which rights talk itself can be seen as a *part* of a broader hegemony. The turn to rights could just as easily suggest a people that have been indoctrinated into an approved and manageable discourse that shapes their expressions of resentment into forms that are subject to the control of the state.

This last debate cannot, of course, be resolved through survey research, but by carrying these questions to an examination of the formal legal battles that grew out of worker opposition to testing, later chapters will try to shed some light on the ramifications of the turn to rights in this particular struggle.

This chapter has two goals beyond that of simply learning about the workers' response to testing: to assess the impact that the drug crisis had on workers and their reactions to testing and to demonstrate and explore the centrality of rights talk. The next section provides an overview of the consenting and resisting factions and how they feel about drug testing. Then, we turn to listen to the workers themselves by looking at the reasons they give for supporting or opposing testing programs. Following that, we look more closely at differences among pro- and antitesting subgroups to explain the perceptual and ideological factors involved in taking a position on this topic. (The survey and its administration are discussed in appendix 1.)

The Views of the Tested

This brief section reports on the basic question whether these skilled workers supported or opposed each of four basic types of drug-testing programs. While a full discussion of the methods and limits of the survey is offered in appendix 1, let me stress that these results on support and opposition should not be viewed as a gauge to the opinions of all American workers. That is not the goal here, and the survey—based in one large union local and unable to eliminate some element of self-selection—is not designed to accomplish it.

That said, note that these results are similar to those found in some of the national and workplace opinion polls taken in the middle to late 1980s. While a 1986 *USA Today* survey found that fully 77 percent of adults—not necessarily workers—did not object to being tested, this same group had a 62 percent to 29 percent split in favor of mandatory testing for federal workers and shifted to 48 percent opposition and 43 percent support when it came to drug testing in private sector firms (Walsh and Trumble 1991). The final figure is almost identical to the general division over testing seen below.

There are four basic testing programs considered here. *Random drug testing* involves selecting a sample from the entire pool of workers; normally, a computer or lottery is used to select those to be tested. Random programs cost less and can have an effect similar to universal testing because workers never know when they might be tested and must therefore act on the assumption of a pending test. *Preemployment testing* involves the screening of all applicants for employment at a company. *Postaccident testing* refers to programs in which employees who have been involved in a workplace accident are tested. *Suspicion-based testing* refers to programs that require the establishment of a reasonable suspicion that an individual is using drugs before a test can be administered.

As table 1 shows, random drug testing is the most strongly opposed type of program with a full 67 percent opposing it and only 24 percent supporting it.[2]

TABLE 1.   Support and Opposition for Four Testing Programs, in Percentage

| | Potential Programs | | | |
	Random	Pre-employment	Post-accident	Suspicion
Oppose	67	43	34	34
Mid	10	12	19	10
Support	24	46	47	56
Total Percentage	101	101	100	100
N	(797)	(783)	(773)	(777)

Those surveyed hold more mixed views on preemployment testing, postaccident testing, and testing based on an individualized suspicion of drug use. Opinion is almost evenly split on preemployment testing—45.5 percent support and 43 percent opposition.[3] Postaccident testing receives about the same degree of support as preemployment (47 percent), but opposition is weaker (34 percent), and a full 19 percent take a middle position. Fifty-five and a half percent of the respondents support testing when an individual is suspected of drug use, while 34 percent are opposed and 10 percent take the middle position.[4]

One of the most important findings here is seen in the difference between programs based on a suspicion of drug use and those based on a random sweep of the work force: more than 55 percent support testing with individual suspicion, yet fully 67 percent oppose random testing. While most of the general opinion surveys merely ask about drug testing, we see here that there is an important difference in worker opinion toward the different testing programs. (Le Roy [1990]) found similar disparities in his survey research among unionized private sector workers.)

One final measure of views on drug-testing programs pertains to whether or not the respondents want the union to oppose drug testing in general. Of those with an opinion, 45 percent want the union to oppose testing, 43 percent want the union to support it, and 12 percent come down in the middle.[5]

Understanding Support and Opposition

Since workers are widely divided on these issues, the obvious question that emerges is, Why? What explains the disagreement? Therefore, our attention turns to a closer look at these countervailing subgroups. In understanding why people feel the way that they do on a topic like this, it is necessary to take account of their beliefs about the severity of the drug problem and the extent to which drug tests threaten or advance values they may hold.

While it could be argued that these perceptual and ideological factors are only spuriously related to views on testing and that more fundamental demographic characteristics and rational interests are the essence of explanation, our knowledge of this population supports the rejection of such arguments. Perhaps the most obvious and oft-heard explanation for opposition to testing is that those who oppose it use illegal drugs and want to avoid apprehension. Although I was unable to ascertain how many among this particular population fall into that category, there are undoubtedly some who do. As seen earlier, however, we know from the results of testing programs in other workplaces that there is a very small percentage of people in a skilled trade who use illegal drugs. Yet a relatively large percentage of these workers oppose testing. In short, there are simply not enough drug users in this population for such an explanation to account for the widespread opposition to testing.

Demographic explanations such as class, age, or education are also unsupported by these data. The amount of variation in opinion among this group of workers—all making roughly the same amount, performing similar trades, and being otherwise similarly placed in the socioeconomic structure—precludes reliance on using class-based arguments for explaining the views of those studies here. If most workers supported testing, or if most workers opposed testing, then it might be appropriate to rely on such arguments in the case at hand, but this condition does not hold. Similarly, age and education seem to have very little to do with views on this topic. There is some tendency for younger respondents to oppose testing more strongly than older ones ($p < .01$), but the association is actually a very weak one ($\tau = .15$).

The failure of these demographic or situational variables turns our attention to the more cultural factors of perception, ideology, and belief. As discussed earlier, the world of social problems, politics, and policy is an ambiguous one to which meaning must be ascribed. Therefore, factors like beliefs about drugs and drug use and values like safety and privacy play a crucial role in sorting competing claims and taking a personal stance. Below, it will be seen that the strongest factors identified in this study have to do with perceptions of the extent of a drug problem and, most importantly, attitudes about privacy, rights, and safety.

Explanations of Positions on Drug Testing

As mentioned above, one of the first portions of the survey involved an open-ended question asking respondents to explain their position on drug testing. In that the issues raised here were not led or introduced by the nature of the question on the survey, they provide the best clues to what is on the minds of the people studied here. "Ideological hegemony," after all, relates to the way that people think; if we are to understand it, explanations and premises must be closely studied in ways that do not twist or lead them. This section begins with a brief overview of the distribution of responses among the workers and then provides a more in-depth look at their views and explanations. For the purposes of this discussion and analysis, the surveyed workers are divided into two main groups: those who want their union to support testing and those who want their union to oppose it.[6]

Of those 290 surveyed workers who want their union to support drug-testing programs and who provide an explanation for their views, the strong majority (65 percent) cite concerns over workplace safety. Twenty percent cite concerns over a general societal drug problem, and 14 percent voice concerns over how the quality and quantity of work was affected by drug use. Some 24 percent of the pro-testing responses were spread out among other less representative responses. The foremost among these were statements that "drugs do not belong in the workplace" (7 percent), that the respondent did not want to work with or be around drug users (4 percent), and that testing could help abusers get treatment (4 percent).[7] (See appendix 1 for a discussion of coding.)

For those 297 who oppose drug testing and provide an explanation, the most important reasons given are concerns over privacy (48 percent), feelings that testing violated some form of specific legal entitlement or right (36 percent), concerns about the possibility of error (28 percent), and concerns about harassment (13 percent). Twenty-seven percent of the antitesting responses fell into smaller groupings, with the foremost being the feeling that drug testing was not a good or necessary strategy (8 percent), was humiliating or degrading (7 percent), or was an unacceptable "one more step" in an increasing pattern of surveillance (5 percent).

The nearly 600 responses to the open-ended question brought a flood of not just specific reasons but observations, statements, and, in a few cases, brief essays on the issues involved in drug-testing debates. Before looking at some comments that portray the feelings and convictions on each side of the issue, consider the words of a few members caught in the middle.

[I] do not like Big Brother looking over my shoulder, yet testing is for all of our safety. (171)[8]

I haven't made my mind up yet. I know mandatory testing would violate my civil rights. Yet as dangerous as this trade can be, can we afford to let alcohol and drug abusers work side by side with us? (299)

I have some real reservations about drug testing on constitutional grounds. I also have an awareness of the seriousness of the drug problem in the U.S.A. When I was a kid in World War Two we made sacrifices, because we felt it was a matter of survival. I feel that the drug problem is serious enough to make some sacrifices now. I will agree to a testing program if the employers are also tested. (243)

For these members, concerns over privacy, rights, safety, and the general drug problem compete; in some ways these individuals therefore express the conflicts within the membership as a whole. But to get a good sense for the strength and nature of the feelings on either side of the divide, we should take a closer look at how they express themselves in their own terms. The comments used below were selected because they represented views that have been more systematically identified within the membership. Knowing that some 65 percent of those who support testing give workplace safety as their reason is a helpful way to summarize population characteristics. But a far more sensitive and meaningful perspective can come from listening to the sentiments and concerns in the words of those most directly involved.

Consent: Supporters of Testing

As noted above, those who support testing programs cite concerns over workplace safety, the national drug problem, the quality and quantity of work performed by drug users, and other issues. These are all values that are important to the workers and were also central features of the attention to illegal drug use among politicians, managers, and the media during the time period preceding the survey (see chaps. 2 and 3).

The percentages given below are as a proportion of the 290 protesting members who explained themselves in the open-ended question. Some of these members simply state, "I have nothing to hide"

(382) or "If you don't use drugs why worry about tests?" (122). But most provide some assessment of the situation or reference to a perceived problem to support their views. Safety is the most oft-cited reason.

Safety: 65 Percent

> I do not feel like being killed by some doper. (675)

> I feel that a great number of industrial accidents are drug related. (576)

> Drug testing for professions involving public safety is warranted. [Our field] also involves situations where sloppy or careless work practices compromise the safety of fellow workers. (158)

> I don't want to die because of someone on drugs. (51)

> I don't want to work with or even be on the job with a person on drugs, I think it is like being on the highway with a drunk, someone will get killed! (8)

> We are dependent on each other in a very good trade. We can cause irreparable harm to ourselves or a partner by not being absolutely alert. Participating in an illegal act is wrong, and why should we support drug cartels who want to enslave us to make money? (285)

The General Drug Problem: 20 Percent

Other respondents, however, base their support of testing on problems they associate with societywide drug use rather than concerns specifically centered in the workplace.

> I feel that drugs are undermining the United States. I feel that people buying drugs should be dealt with just like the pushers. I feel that drug testing will keep people from using drugs. If you don't have a job you can't buy drugs. (769)

Drug use is reaching too far and must be stopped before it completely destroys our country. (659)

Drug testing could retard the spread of crime and 'AIDS'. (504)

I'm opposed to any drug culture. (404)

#1 Drugs are illegal. #2 Drugs should not be used period. (109)

Illegal drugs means illegal and should be punished as far as the law allows. (29)

Productivity: 14 Percent

Another portion of the membership tends to center its support for drug testing on concerns over productivity, while a few, like the third person quoted below, combine their concern over productivity with more general sentiments about drug use and morality.

As union members we represent the very best and most qualified workmen in the industry. This must be the first and foremost in everyone's mind. We cannot tolerate the use of drugs which adds to the demise of our craftsmanship and quality of work. (204)

I support drug testing. People I've known that do regular use of drugs are a problem at work. Someone has to carry their workload. (135)

Drug use is wicked and very unproductive. (70)

Elimination of Drug Users from the Workplace: 10 Percent

It is fairly likely that many of the responses in this category are related to concerns over safety and productivity although they don't make specific reference to those issues. Rather, what we see here is a normally very brief statement about the undesirability of those who use illegal drugs.

I do not use drugs or alcohol of any types and I don't want to work around anyone who does. (320)

I do not use drugs. [I] support programs that would keep me from having to work [with] and be around people who do use drugs. (359)

[I] would not work with a drug user. (320)

Treatment: 4 Percent

Responses here center on concern for the people with drug or alcohol problems rather than for safety, productivity, or other issues.

It could help some people who need help. (193)

Drug testing is ok if used to help people get a hold of their drug problem. I think it should be used to help people overcome the drug situation by requiring them to take drug treatment and go to support groups. But if it's used for termination of personnel only then I think it's wrong because it doesn't help society as a whole. (233)

Opponents of Testing

The arguments and positions of those members who oppose drug testing incorporate a wide variety of concerns including ones over privacy and autonomy, spreading surveillance, legal rights, dignity, harassment, accuracy, and class politics, as well as views that testing is either unneeded or ineffective.

This section conveys the views held by the people who want their union to oppose testing. Percentages given with each classification are as a proportion of the 297 people who provided written explanations. The pattern that emerges here and is confirmed in the statistical analysis in the following section suggests that explicit claims to legal rights to privacy and due process are a very important facet of the oppositional ideology.

Privacy: 48 Percent

It is an invasion of privacy, unconstitutional, and an o.k. to open the door to true programming of people and their private lives. (458)

Is it any of your business? Do you floss? Do you enjoy sex? Why not? Does the person who signs my check drink? Smoke? Fuck? *Well?* (779)

My urine is my biz. (284)

[It's] one more rule to govern people's behavior. I demand the right to control my own life. (202)

[I] have never used any drugs, but do not want to be subjected to outsiders' judgment on whether I should be tested or [on the] outcome. (18)

What I do in the privacy of my own home is my business. If I want to smoke a joint once a month (at home) I shouldn't be penalized at work. (89)

Explicit Legal Arguments: 36 Percent

The views offered under this heading represent those who explicitly call forth some legalistic principle in their opposition.[9]

It's against the Constitution. (184)

[Drug testing] violates our constitutional rights to privacy and our protection from self-incrimination (4th & 5th amend.), [and] undermines the constitution itself. (83)

Although I strongly oppose illegal drugs and agree something must be done, I feel this is a criminal problem. Testing for all is a further loss of rights and subject to humiliation, mistakes and abuse for those who live within the law. I cannot accept any promise that this will not happen. (411)

This is America! *The* country where a person is innocent until proven guilty *in a court of law only* after charges are *filed*. What happened to due process? (265)

Testing Error: 27 Percent

The concern addressed here is the possibility of error.

I am against any program that could possibly give *false test results* and this is my main concern. (347)

I don't like the idea of taking aspirin and coming up positive, then either being fired or having to defend yourself for no good reason. (360)

No drug test is 100 percent sure. (244)

Harassment or Discrimination: 13 Percent

Statements falling into this category expressed a fear about the use of drug tests to harass individuals.

I believe drug testing "randomly chosen" [workers] or "suspects" could be used as harassment or [to] "get even." (85)

I fear that a "testing" program will be used as a punitive measure against "certain" persons—mouthy [ones or] boat rockers. . . . What should be considered as a medical problem has tended to become, due to current federal government administration, a method of marking out undesirables. (263)

I feel random testing is a new means of employee harassment. If this happens unfavored employees will be tested three times a week [and] favorites not at all. (616)

Unnecessary or Ineffective Policy: 8 Percent

For different reasons, some simply don't think that testing is necessary and others question its effectiveness.

I don't see drug use as a large problem in our industry. I think we need to address other problems far ahead of drugs (i.e. organizing [and] more money). (537)

I haven't found drugs to be bad in the work place and I don't want the bother or nuisance of such tests. (470)

I am a recovering addict. I would in no way get help to quit if I was forced to. (449)

There has been no real educational effort in the workplace. Let's identify the solutions for this problem in society and treat it, not just force people out of a job. (98)

I believe drug testing by an employer gives them the opportunity to abuse that power. I believe that if employees, employers and union work together the problem can be solved without resort to drug testing. We all pretty much know who the drug users are. They need to be confronted and helped *if possible*. (27)

Dignity: 7 Percent

A number of those opposed to drug testing argued that it was a humiliating affront to human dignity.

I think it's humiliating to have to urinate into a vial while someone is observing you. (26)

The drug testing of employees is tantamount to an assault on the intrinsic dignity of a human being. (392)

It is a degradation of human beings, Damn You. (500)

I believe that the possibility of mistakes is very high, but most importantly, I feel that it is degrading and humiliating to enact such a policy. [It] empowers the employer to subject you to that degradation and humiliation even if you have *never* given them the slightest cause to suspect you of drug use or abuse. (22)

Surveillance: 5 Percent

Others link their opposition to drug testing to broader concerns over monitoring and surveillance in society.

> Where does it stop? Would they test for alcohol? Picture a hot . . . summer night. You just mowed the lawn. Perspiration rolls from your brow. Should you quench your thirst with a beer? (673)

> While I don't object to a drug free workplace, I feel that drug testing is an unwarranted intrusion on individual rights. Also I think it opens the door to other types of medical screening. For instance, genetic testing for insurance or employment to determine predispositions to various weaknesses or maladies. (294)

> I feel that drug testing would only give Big Brother another window into your life. (62)

> [It is an] invasion of privacy and it's unconstitutional, also what's next, our sex habits and who (racially speaking) we are married to[?] (47)

> [The] next step might be a microphone in my bedroom. (526)

Not Performance Related: 2 Percent

Sharing the view of many forensic scientists, a small number of respondents point out that drug tests don't measure actual job performance and that they therefore are not a legitimate tool for management to use.

> What a person does off the job site is none of my business. All that should matter is job performance. (251)

> I feel that a worker should be judged by his or her work and nothing else. (244)

It enables employee supervisors to terminate employees *for some-thing other than poor job performance,* and enables employers to blame accidents on *something other than poor job conditions.* (5 per-cent of accidents are drug related, but they would love to blame all accidents on drugs. It cuts down their liability). (3)

I do not feel that the employer has the right to control what an employee does when not at work. Doing drugs may affect their work performance, but the drugs shouldn't be an issue, the work performance should. (569)

Class Politics: 2 Percent

A tiny portion of those opposed to testing state their opposition in terms of class or labor-management conflict.

Working class people will suffer more. They always have and they always will!!!! (360)

[Drug testing] gives employers excessive power which can and will and *is* being used to control and victimize "undesirable" workers and is the worst UNION BUSTING weapon yet devised. (83)

Privacy, Rights, and the Drug Crisis: Explaining Positions on Testing

In the effort to learn more about the nature of beliefs toward drug testing, respondents were asked a series of questions about issues that had been raised in the controversies over drug testing. The pre-ceding section noted the role that impressions of the national drug crisis, threats to safety, and infringements on privacy and other rights seem to play in shaping the face of consent and resistance. If we go by sheer numerical weight, the standoff here is between safety and the drug crisis, on the one hand, and privacy and due process on the other. This section follows up on these themes through a statistical analysis of the role that these factors play in shaping the workers' responses to testing: it shows that the sheer numerical weight approach just touched upon does a pretty good, but not perfect, job of telling us what the important relationships are.

The Drug Crisis

Edelman (1977, 1988), Hall et al. (1978), and others have argued that when a public perceives a crisis that threatens them or their nation, they are likely to behave differently than they might otherwise behave. The crisis—whether a drug crisis, an oil crisis, a street crime crisis, or a foreign policy crisis—has been increasingly viewed as, inter alia, one part of an array of means through which authorities create or maintain their dominance (Hall et al. 1978). They can, in Edelman's words, serve to "justify the actions of leaders and the sacrifices leaders demand of others" (1977, 44).

Implicit in this argument is the belief that a crisis can override the interests and perceptions of a public such that citizens accept assessments and policies that they might not otherwise agree with. The analysis that follows largely affirms this view but also shows that personal assessments of the local manifestations of broad public problems, as well as beliefs relating to values such as rights and privacy, can have a significant mitigating effect on the impact of a crisis campaign.

TABLE 2.   Assessments of the Drug Problem in the Nation and the Workplace by percentage

| | Assessment of Drug Problem | | | | |
	Crisis	Near Crisis	Mid	Near No Problem	No Real Problem
Levels of Assessment					
Nation	56.7 (453)	22.5 (180)	12.4 (99)	3.5 (28)	4.9 (39)
Workplace	10.9 (84)	15.2 (117)	22.8 (175)	16.3 (125)	34.8 (267)

Note: Cells show percentage holding such views; n in parentheses.

Table 2 leaves no doubt that most of those surveyed here perceive a national drug crisis. The striking majority concur with the
assessments of the media and public officials that the "nation faces a
crisis over illegal drugs." On the other hand, when members were
asked about the extent of illegal drug use *within their own workplace*,
the outcome was quite different—slightly more than half lean toward
saying that drug use is "not a real problem," while about a quarter
feel that drug use in their workplace approaches crisis proportions.

Thus we see a good deal of difference between assessments of
the problem at the local and national level. Which assessment is more
important in affecting the respondent's views on drug testing? Is it
the national drug crisis that had been emphasized in elections and
news programs for more than four years prior to this survey? Or is it
their assessment of conditions within their own workplace? The latter
setting, presumably, is where the most proximate justification for
testing would be found; it is here where their interests in safety reside
and where workers are less dependent on distant and constructed
images of public problems. This question, therefore, provides a good
check on the validity of arguments holding that the national crisis
mentality can override local perception and interest.

The figures presented in table 3 display a subgroup's mean rating
on a scale measuring whether or not they want their union to (1)
support or (5) oppose drug-testing programs. By controlling for the
respondents' assessments of the drug problem at the national and
workplace levels (1 = crisis, 2 = moderate, 3 = not a real problem),
it is possible to explore the interplay of these assessments in helping
to explain their views.[10] Can a national crisis generate support for
workplace testing among people who see no real problem in their
own place of employment? The answer is, not surprisingly, yes and
no. As expected, for those who perceive both a national and a
workplace crisis, support for testing is a very strong 1.95 (recall that
the scale is from 1 to 5, not 0 to 5). Similarly, for those who see no
drug problem at either level of assessment, mean opposition to drug
testing is a very strong 4.4.

The relationships seen here show that both the national crisis
assessment ($p < .001$) and the local assessment ($p < .001$) have a
significant effect on people's responses to drug-testing initiatives.
But the workers' assessments of conditions within their own daily
lives clearly outweigh the media imagery put forth at the national

level. The squared Eta scores[11] show that the assessment of the local workplace situation (.17) is more strongly related to support and opposition to drug testing than the national assessment (.11). While these findings confirm the powerful effect that a sense of national crisis can have, they also show the importance of personal experience and assessment in the daily lives of the citizenry.

Concerns about Drug Tests

The preceding pages addressed the combined effects of different and often competing assessments of the drug problem in influencing the respondent's views on drug testing. We saw that workers will often reject a national crisis mentality and related policy impositions if their sense of their own daily reality conflicts with the broader imagery and agenda. A parallel set of concerns is considered here, where we look at the ways in which workers' opinions on the impact and appropriateness of drug testing itself shape their positions.

The debates over drug testing in both the press and the courts, while stressing the drug crisis, also return to questions over whether

TABLE 3. Positions on Drug Testing as Affected by Assessments of Drug Problems in the Nation and the Workplace[a]

Assessment of Drug Problem in Nation[c]		Assessment of Drug Problem in Workplace[b]			
		Crisis	Mid	No Problem	Nation Means
	Crisis	1.95 (185)	2.54 (141)	3.41 (250)	2.73 (576)
	Mid	1.00 (1)	3.86 (29)	4.17 (64)	4.04 (94)
	No Problem	3.75 (4)	4.00 (2)	4.41 (54)	4.41 (60)
Workplace Means		1.98 (190)	2.78 (172)	3.69 (368)	

[a]Cell entries show mean position on drug testing: 1 = strong support, 5 = strong opposition; n in parentheses. Overall main effect: $F = (8,721) = 25.33$, $p < .001$, and $R^2 = .22$.
[b]Effect of workplace assessment: $F (2,721) = 47.77$, $p < .001$ and Eta Squared $= .17$.
[c]Effect of national assessment: $F (2,721) = 22.23$, $p < .001$ and Eta Squared $= .11$.

or not drug tests violate constitutional rights, invade privacy, or are subject to error. Some of the crisis literature would suggest that even those who were concerned about such issues might be willing to overlook them in the face of a perceived crisis, but this belief may erroneously downplay the importance of values and interests that compete with suggested policies.

To gain a systematic measurement of whether or not individuals felt that drug testing raises concerns over privacy, rights, accuracy, and other issues, we asked them to note whether they agreed or disagreed with a number of statements that "different people" have made about drug testing. Table 4 provides an overview of the ques-

TABLE 4. Responses to Pro- and Antitesting Statements, Problem Assessments, and Relation of Views to Desired Union Policy

	Percentage			Correlation with Policy Preference (r)	N
	Agree	Mid	Disagree		
Employee drug testing . . .					
violates constitutional rights.	51	14	35	.79	746
gives too much power to employers.	54	17	29	.77	759
is an invasion of privacy.	54	12	34	.75	772
improves workplace productivity.	31	20	50	.60	720
improves workplace safety.	57	19	24	.58	745
helps drug abusers get treatment.	51	22	27	.50	728
is likely to make mistakes.	63	24	13	.40	721
	Crisis	Mid	Not a Real Problem		
Drugs in the nation are	79	12	8	.36	767
Drugs in my workplace are	26	23	51	.42	736

aPolicy preferences were measured by whether a respondent wanted the union to oppose or support testing programs. While this table shows a three-way breakdown for the response percentages, the correlation coefficient (Pearson's r) was calculated using the original five-point scale. All relations are in the intuitively obvious direction. (See appendix 1.)

tions, the responses, and the relationship between these issues and support or opposition to testing. Responses were entered on a five-point scale with a "Don't Know" option set to the right of the scale. Here, responses have been collapsed to a three-point scale (agree, middle, disagree),[12] "Don't Knows" have been excluded, and the correlation coefficient expressing the relationship between the variable and overall views on testing is shown at the right. Statements are ordered by the strength of correlation, not their appearance in the survey form.

The correlation coefficients express the strength of the relationship between workers' views on specific aspects of testing and the overall question whether they want their union to support or oppose testing. These figures show that the issues of privacy, rights, and power are more strongly associated with a position on testing than other widely discussed issues like the possibility of testing error. And while 57 percent feel that testing will improve safety, it ranks relatively low as a factor associated with their basic decision about testing (perhaps because many who feel that it may improve safety still oppose it for these other reasons).

While fully 63 percent feel that tests are likely to make mistakes, this issue is apparently a relatively weak one in their overall decision given the correlation and its rank in the open-ended portion of the survey. As will be seen in the following chapter, much of the legal activity over drug testing (i.e., judicial opinions, law review articles, etc.) centers on the issue of accuracy. Debates here turn on whether the tests are or can be mistake free enough to pass a fairness muster. But here we see that the issues of rights and privacy are far more important to the workers. In that most legal success has been centered on improving accuracy rather than protecting privacy (see chap. 5), the workers' real concerns are neither well expressed nor enacted. Indeed, since a high degree of accuracy is often concomitant to the judicial approving of testing programs, the focus on accuracy may work against resistance to testing.

Managing Public Opinion? Rights, Privacy, and the
Drug Crisis

Concerns over privacy and rights were the most frequently expressed reasons for opposing drug testing in the open-ended portion of the survey. The associations seen here between opposition to testing and the belief that testing is an invasion of privacy and a violation of constitutional rights confirm the centrality of legal claims.

These results show that while the perception of a national drug crisis is a significant factor in understanding support and opposition to drug testing, assessments of the drug problem within one's own workplace and views on whether or not drug testing invades privacy and violates rights are of greater importance.[13] As was seen in studying the relationships between national and local drug problem assessments, the power of crises to shape public reactions should not be overestimated. The cultural proclivity to assert claims to rights and values significantly mitigates the national crisis mentality; hence, it would be a serious error to discount these factors.[14]

These results both confirm and temper theoretical work on the ability of national crises to sway publics to accept burdens; crises can sway publics, but personal experience, commitments to legal rights and cultural values, and concerns about the drawbacks of proposed policy responses create important limits. The final chapter takes up a discussion of how these findings relate to broader debates over the question of ideological hegemony.

The Turn to Rights

As seen, concerns over privacy, constitutional rights, the danger of testing error, and the possibility of discrimination or harassment under testing programs make up the main body of opposition arguments. While there are obviously a number of facets to these expressions of resistance to testing, claims that are either explicitly or implicitly drawn from the legal culture dominate their explanations.[15] The language of rights is, as Edwards, Foucault, and others would expect, the main vocabulary of opposition to drug testing.[16] This sense of unanimity is quite significant.

The "class politics" category, the argument that testing will be ineffective, or the linking of testing to broader patterns of surveillance, for example, are all straightforward and important critiques of testing programs. In some ways, they might even seem more effective or meaningful than a rights-based argument, but they are found among a minority of those who oppose testing. The significance of this general agreement that *the* issue is rights, is further illuminated by looking at a relevant critique of testing that is, apparently, not the issue: power. When the survey raised this concern by asking whether testing "gives too much power to employers," fully 54 percent of the workers agreed, and their positions were strongly linked to their stance on testing. But the concern about power is essentially a nonissue in the uncued portion of the survey where only a handful of respondents brought it up. Power, apparently, was not on the workers' minds until somebody else raised the issue.

Following many critics of cued survey questions, one could thus argue that the power question had measured a nonopinion—an issue that was not salient until the survey raised it. In this case, that is precisely the point of interest. All these people, who were ready to see this as a power issue when asked, had instead framed their complaints in the formal, official language of rights.[17] Theoretically, the language of power is no less—and arguably more—appropriate than the language of rights in the controversy at hand. After all, a person who can invade your privacy, deny your autonomy, and compel you to urinate in a jar could clearly be considered as having too much power in your life. Yet it is the language of rights, not power, through which antitesting concerns are expressed. One effect of the centrality of the rights discourse is that it masks or displaces a way of thinking and speaking that would more directly confront the political problem in this setting—an imbalance of power between the bosses and their workers.

The cultural politics and momentum that lead to the almost universal turn to rights among those who oppose testing is, in important ways, as significant, constraining, and potentially subjugating as the sense of threat and crisis that pervades the thoughts of those who support testing. We just saw the issue of power is as important and as present, though latently, as the rights-based critique of testing. Yet virtually no workers brought it up on their own. Hundreds, and nationally millions, of distinct and differently situated individuals confronted with an issue like drug testing turn to the same small vocabulary to express themselves. This amorphous process of cultural convergence is of massive importance in the shaping and resolution of private perception and public conflict.

What, then, are the implications of this turn to rights? Some are clear. Rights claims add a certain legitimation and cultural clout to a policy position that might otherwise be seen as a "soft on drugs" or even prodrug stance. In terms of formal legal processes, they imply a venue of conflict and a system of adjudication and conflict resolution that is capable of producing significant victories for opponents of government or workplace policies.

But with such resources come costs and potential costs. One is the displacement of conceptualizations and responses that are outside the apparent discourse of rights—such as the issue of power discussed above (see Tushnet 1984; chap. 1). More tactically, the move to the legal terrain will probably displace grass roots action and structure as lawyers and lawsuits move to the forefront of campaigns (McCann 1986). And the converse of the possibility of legal victory discussed in the preceding paragraph is the possibility of defeat. The law may be ambiguous and contingent, but judges still rule (see Carter and Gilliom 1989), and they may well rule against you. Obviously, resources and constraints are crosscutting and will vary from context to context; to understand the implications of the turn to the famous formal right in this setting, the next chapter takes a close look at how some of the most important legal conflicts over testing have played out.

Chapter 5

The Courts: Privacy,
Due Process, and the
Fourth Amendment

My private life is my private life.
—Craftsman, age 47, 1989

In limited circumstances, where the privacy interests implicated by the search are minimal, and where an important government interest furthered by the intrusion would be placed in jeopardy by a requirement of individualized suspicion, a search may be reasonable despite the absence of suspicion. We believe this is true of the intrusions in question here.
—Justice Anthony Kennedy,
Skinner v. Railway Labor Executives' Association

Rights to privacy and due process are most typically on the minds of those who oppose drug testing. The emergence of such language is hardly surprising because testing challenges so many facets of these values: it requires urination on demand and often under direct observation, it inquires into previously shielded areas of life, it compels the provision of personal medical information, and it denies individuals control over their off-duty time. Further, on the due process front, careers hang in the balance with the possibility of false test results or the employers' potential abuse of the power manifest in testing.

This chapter offers an overview of how the courts have responded to the antitesting claims of American workers in some of the leading federal cases over public sector testing. Judges' efforts to make sense of these areas of the law have produced widespread disagreement and contradiction. Some opinions have been wholesale endorsements of the antitesting arguments seen in the preceding chapter. Other judges, however, discount and reject the antitesting critique at almost every turn. They weaken the Fourth Amendment claims of workers by placing drug tests in the category of "administrative searches" that meet "special needs" of the government relating to safety, security, or workplace management. Then, by "balancing" the rights of the individual against the needs of the government, it is ruled that the drug-testing programs in question are not unreasonable searches.

This chapter culminates with a critical assessment of the Supreme Court rulings on drug-testing programs in the Customs Agency and the rail industry. It will be argued that the Supreme Court's rulings in favor of mandatory drug testing reflect more than just a minimizing of privacy concerns; they rely on a logic of social control that shares and actively supports the goals and assumptions of generalized surveillance programs. In short, the approach to social control that drives the drug-testing initiative also drives the Supreme Court majority's legal reasoning on drug-testing cases.

While it will be up to future historians to tell us how these issues are finally resolved, I will argue that the trend revealed by the Supreme Court's decisions shows that formal legal opposition to testing falls far short of being the meaningful avenue of resistance that the image of law and the dignity of the rights claim often imply. It is, rather, colonized by actors and ideologies that overrun the antitesting movement. If this viewpoint prevails, it will be argued, it is certain that labor unions will continue to lose cases, as has been the trend in the few years following the Court's rulings (Lewis 1990). More broadly, such a change may also signal a basic reorientation in the legal organization of social control in American society.[1]

An American Tradition? Privacy Rights in the Fourth Amendment

The Fourth Amendment is the most specific recognition of the right to privacy in the Constitution.
                                                                    —C. Herman Pritchett

Privacy is not mentioned in the Constitution. It may have approached such a status when, in the 1960s and early 1970s, Supreme Court cases such as *Griswold v. Connecticut* and *Roe v. Wade* were decided on the basis of a constitutional right to privacy understood to be implicit in the Bill of Rights (Copelon 1989). However, this version of the right to privacy has been largely limited to situations involving the sex lives of heterosexuals and their decisions about family and procreation. Not surprisingly, therefore, federal appellate courts have said little about this right in their decisions on drug testing (Bible 1989, 690–91; see the discussion in *McDonnel v. Hunter*).[2] But the courts have said a great deal about privacy; they do so within the search and seizure framework of the Fourth Amendment. Since a search is, by its nature and legal definition, an encroachment on privacy, Fourth Amendment law unavoidably deals with this concern.[3]

Bookspan argues that Americans have "long recognized the need to maintain a zone of privacy to protect the individual from the roving eye of government and fellow citizens" (1987, 309). This recognition is, in part, expressed in the British and American search and seizure laws that were developed in reaction to the tactics of the Star Chamber and those of the British authorities in the American colonies. The emergent legal provisions worked to prohibit the general warrants and writs of assistance that were used through the middle and late eighteenth century; these allowed authorities to search any residence or business in seeking those guilty of treason, sedition, tax evasion, or other crimes.

Like contemporary drug-testing programs that rely on random or postaccident testing, the king's searches were not based on suspicion that an individual had done anything wrong.[4] Because of this lack of a basis, they constituted an ongoing threat to the privacy of the general public—the possibility of a search was ever-present, and life had to be lived with the expectation of a visit from the royal troops. Therefore, the threat of the search itself worked as an ongoing means of disciplining the population.

The antisearch reaction in both British common law and the American constitutional movement resulted in a privacy-protecting requirement that searches could not be conducted absent a warrant and that warrants must be based on probable cause and specifically name the person and place to be searched (Bookspan 1987, 316–20). The basis of this requirement was laid in the state declarations of rights in the 1770s and incorporated into the Fourth Amendment of the federal Bill of Rights in 1789.

The right of the people to be secure in their persons, houses, papers, and effects against unreasonable searches and seizures shall not be violated, and no Warrants shall issue, but upon probable cause, supported by Oath or affirmation, and particularly describing the place to be searched, and the persons or things to be seized.

An early draft of the amendment had a single provision:

The rights of the people to be secured in their persons, houses, papers, and effects, shall not be violated by warrants issued without probable cause, supported by oath or affirmation and not particularly describing the place to be searched and the persons or things to be seized. (Bookspan 1987, 320 n.71)

In this version it is the general search that is prohibited, and there is little ambiguity about what the framers meant. But, in the version that made it into the Constitution, it is the "unreasonable search" that is prohibited, and it is not necessarily clear that the second clause regarding warrants and probable cause is meant to provide the definition of the reasonable search. Judges are therefore presented with the necessarily creative and political lawmaking process of deciding what is meant by "unreasonable." Some rely on the amendment's second clause and argue that in all but the most extreme circumstances, the warrantless search, or one made in the absence of probable cause,[5] is per se unreasonable. Others increasingly separate the two clauses of the Fourth Amendment and argue that the warrantless search is not necessarily unreasonable; the context of the search must be taken into consideration in deciding what is or is not reasonable.

From the former approach, only such things as the potential for immediate danger to an officer or the ability of a suspect to rapidly transport the items to be searched could override the requirement of a search warrant. But the latter approach—"enjoying a renaissance particularly in the opinions of Chief Justice Rehnquist" (Bookspan 1987, 332–33)—separates the two provisions and holds that the warrant is only one means to protect the people against unreasonable searches, not an absolute requirement of the reasonable search. Under this logic, a general search or a warrantless search may be fully acceptable if it is "reasonable" in light of the judge's analysis of the context in which the search took place. Many of the cases over employee drug testing have pivoted on how a judge approaches the question of reasonableness. As will be seen later, it is a central dividing line on the Supreme Court.

Suspicionless testing programs—random, universal, preemployment, or postaccident—are necessarily done without a warrant or the element of individualized suspicion that is at the heart of the warrant requirement. If the Fourth Amendment grew out of the threat to privacy manifest in the general warrants of the seventeenth and eighteenth centuries, it has most strongly protected that privacy by requiring that specific warrants or, at least, reasonable suspicions be held by those conducting the search (see also Kamisar 1987). Such a requirement is a safeguard for privacy because the state must show good reason to search *before* it searches. Therefore, it cannot deploy its considerable powers of surveillance unless articulable reasons for suspicion arise through other means. Certainly privacy will be invaded once that suspicion has arisen, but the use of a standing system of wide social surveillance such as suspicionless drug tests would be unacceptable.

But if one only asks that a search be "reasonable" within a broad context including factors such as the nature of the institutional setting, the specific characteristics of the search, the type of employment involved, and a cost-benefit analysis of the challenged policy, then— as seen below—it is easier to make the Fourth Amendment support standing systems of surveillance.

Privacy and the Fourth Amendment in the Drug-testing Cases

The claims of workers who oppose testing were advanced in dozens of federal cases challenging the constitutionality of drug-testing programs.[6] The issue of privacy emerges in every drug-testing case because the degree of invasion manifest in a search is central to contemporary Fourth Amendment analysis. It is critical in deciding whether a search has occurred,[7] in deciding whether a search will be classified as administrative or criminal, and in deciding whether government interests outweigh the privacy rights of the individual. Due process questions also appear in every drug-testing case because of the ever-present concerns over testing accuracy and fairness in the selection of those to be tested.

As seen in chapter 4, these issues are also central to an understanding of how surveyed workers approached questions surrounding drug testing. The definition and measurement of a privacy invasion is, therefore, central to how both workers and judges frame and explain their feelings about testing. It is here that we find one of the most direct and important intersections between these groups.

The pages that follow discuss opinions and arguments that both support and reject antitesting claims on the issues of privacy and due process. I begin with an overview of the diverse ways in which judges addressed the different dimensions of privacy and due process in the federal court decisions preceding the Supreme Court rulings in *National Treasury Employees Union v. von Raab* and *Skinner v. Railway Labor Executives' Association*. The discussion of each dimension begins with workers' statements expressing the antitesting arguments in their own terms. As is undoubtedly necessary when many claims are brought together in an institutionally embedded legal discussion performed by a judge, the views are not always accepted in a direct manner or expressed in their own terms. In some cases, it seems that the gist of the opposition's claims remains vibrantly alive. In others, however, any resemblance between the complaint and the legal cognizance of it is elusive. Generally something called *privacy* is recognized, and sometimes it takes the day. Increasingly, however, redefinitions of the nature or importance of privacy, or the mitigation of privacy claims by special needs or circumstances, serve to reject these oppositional claims.

The Dimensions of Privacy

In an 1890 *Harvard Law Review* article entitled "The Right to Privacy," Louis Brandeis and his partner Samuel Warren quoted Judge Cooley in describing privacy as the right "'to be let alone'" (Warren and Brandeis 1890, 195). Citing "recent inventions and business methods," they feared that new technologies would soon mean that "what is whispered in the closet shall be proclaimed from the house-tops" (Warren and Brandeis 1890, 195). Years later, in the classic surveillance case of *Olmstead v. United States*, Brandeis described privacy as "the most comprehensive of rights and the right most valued by civilized men" (277 U.S. at 438).

Privacy is a word with many meanings. The contemporary idea builds from this "right to be let alone" to center on individuals' control over the sharing of information about themselves. This information includes personal data such as medical reports or information about what one does behind closed doors. It also covers the exposure of the body and what are often called, after all, the "private parts" (see Westin 1967, 7–22). Further, many argue that the concept of privacy also includes the idea of autonomy—the right to make decisions free of authoritative control (Copelon 1989, 298–300; Westin 1967). Each of these dimensions of privacy was evident in the survey of workers faced with drug-testing programs, and each played an important part in the explanations of those who oppose testing.

Dignity and Visual Privacy

I feel it is an invasion of my body and morals to line up in front of a sani–can with a cup.
—Craftswoman, age unknown (793)

I think it's humiliating to have to urinate into a vial while someone is observing you.
—Craftsman, age 41 (26)

I just don't like the idea of having to perform a bodily function for somebody else's satisfaction.
—Craftsman, age 34 (723)

Few have argued that compelled urination in the aural or visual presence of another is not an act that raises significant concerns about human privacy and dignity. Indeed, urine testing has attracted much attention because it often involves the observed performance of something that we do quite often but normally in private and at the risk of arrest in public. "Excreting body fluids and body wastes is one of the most personal and private human functions" (*McDonnel v. Hunter*, 612 F. Supp. at 1127). As the widely cited statement of the circuit court in *National Treasury Employees Union v. von Raab* put it,

There are few activities in our society more personal or private than the passing of urine. Most people describe it by euphemisms if they talk about it at all. It is a function traditionally performed without public observation; indeed, its performance in public is generally prohibited by law as well as social custom. (816 F.2d at 175)

But the perceived threat to dignity and visual privacy varies widely in the courts. Some judges have ruled that a urine test is as invasive as a body cavity search, given the degradation and invasion manifest in each type of search (*McDonnel v. Hunter*, 612 F. Supp. at 1127). Others have ruled that drug tests are "less intrusive than body cavity and strip searches" (*Shoemaker v. Handel*, 619 F. Supp. at 1101). Still others argue that "drug testing . . . is even more intrusive than a search of the home . . . . [It has a] massive intrusive effect" (*von Raab*, 649 F. Supp. at 386–87). Obviously there is a lot of disagreement over the intrusiveness of a drug test; not surprisingly, those judges whose rhetoric suggests a sense of great intrusion have tended to oppose testing, and those who describe it as a minimal check or a normal medical procedure tend to support it.

Informational Privacy

[I oppose testing] because once they have the test medium (urine) to begin with nothing prevents testing for other drugs. If an employer was choosing between applicants would you want your (potential) employer to know if you were taking, by legal prescription, hypertensive drugs . . . , anti-depressants, muscle relaxants, *any* drug you and your doctor have decided is beneficial to you.
—Craftsman, age 42 (212)

Testing will turn up *medication* which could make an employer reluctant to have you as an employee. (Diabetes, high blood pressure, heart problems, etc.)
—Craftsperson, age unknown (515)

Drug testing also involves the retrieval of medical information that is widely respected as confidential (see relevant opinions in, for example, *McDonnel*, 809 F.2d at 1307; *Shoemaker*, 795 F.2d at 1141; *Policeman's Benevolent Association of New Jersey Local 318 v. Washington Township*, 672 F. Supp. at 784; *Lovvorn v. City of Chattanooga*, 647 F. Supp.

at 879; *Capua v. City of Plainfield*, 643 F. Supp. at 1513). Several judges
have pointed out that a urine test is a search that is almost unlimited
in its ability to reveal private medical information; epilepsy, heart
conditions, current medications, and pregnancy can all be revealed.
Indeed, the Washington, D.C., Police Department was so taken with
these capabilities that it secretly analyzed the drug-test samples of its
female employees for signs of pregnancy (*Washington Post*, November
5, 1987, A1). As Judge Sarokin put it,

> Both blood and urine can be analyzed in a medical laboratory to
> discover numerous physiological facts about the person from
> whom it came, including, but not limited to recent ingestion of
> drugs or alcohol. (*Capua*, 643 F. Supp. at 1513)

Drug-testing programs also gather medical information beyond
that revealed through urinalysis; those who are tested are normally
required to fill out a form listing all prescription and nonprescription
medication used in the recent past. That is because of the extensive
problem of false positives—when a prescription or licit nonprescription drug appears on the test as heroin, marijuana, or some other
illegal drug. Although this information may provide some protection
against faulty drug tests, it does so by significantly increasing the
invasion of informational privacy. Many judges have required this
listing of medication as part of a due process effort to make sure that
drug tests are as accurate as possible in identifying illegal drug users.
Ironically, then, this due process provision increases and advances
the privacy violations manifest in urinalysis.

Most judges have not dwelled on the question of informational
privacy once procedural safeguards have been set up to prevent the
divulgence of the information to persons not involved in the administration of the drug-testing program. When such safeguards have not
been explicit, as in *Capua*, judges have shown strong concern. But as
the procedural regulations become pro forma, judges increasingly
decline to discuss the issue, or they simply note that safeguards
against publicization are adequate (see *Shoemaker*, 619 F. Supp. at
1106–7).

However, critics raise two points that procedures can never displace. First is the issue of human error and breaks in the chain of
custody; while the regulations appear fool- and cad-proof, we know

from human experience that such is never the case (see chap. 3;
Fogel, Kornblut, and Porter 1988, 593; Miller 1986, 207). Second is a
broader concern that the zone of informational privacy is not drawn
around the individual or around the individual and a personal doctor,
family members, or living partners. Rather the zone of privacy is
drawn around the individual and the U.S. government or the individual and his or her employer. This broad definition of informational
privacy certainly strains some authors' conceptions of the individual's "personal space" (see especially Westin 1967).

Autonomy

I demand the right to control my own life.
                                    —Craftsman, age unknown (202)

I believe the employers should not be able to tell me what to do
on my off duty hours.
                                    —Craftsman, age 39 (604)

I feel that my time away from work is my time, and what I do with
my time is personal as long as it doesn't interfere with my work
performance and job safety.
                                    —Craftsman, age unknown (155)

A good deal of attention has been directed at a problem created by
the current state of technology in the drug-testing industry. Urine
tests are unable to establish when a drug was taken; even if they
correctly identify the drug, all that is known is that drug use occurred
at some point in the past. In the case of marijuana, Morgan (1987)
had one experimental subject who produced positive results for more
than sixty days following exposure. Other drugs have shorter lives;
ironically, cocaine, the culprit of the War on Drugs, is one of the
most fleeting and therefore most difficult to detect.

The point of concern here is that while drug-testing programs are
largely explained in terms of on-the-job safety and productivity, urine
testing says nothing about current impairment. Urinalysis is such a
wide and unspecific sweep that it unavoidably regulates off-the-job
behavior. The model employee who smokes marijuana on the week-
end is indistinguishable from a chronic pothead. This puts employers
in the position of dictating lifestyle standards to their employees

twenty-four hours a day and therefore raises the concerns over autonomy, as seen in the quotations above and in the following excerpt from *Capua v. City of Plainfield:*

> Drug testing is a form of surveillance, albeit a technological one. Nonetheless, it reports on a person's off-duty activities just as surely as someone had been present and watching. It is George Orwell's "Big Brother" Society come to life. (643 F. Supp. at 1511)

There are obviously a number of tensions between that cluster of values we call privacy and the general thrust of an employee drug-testing program. Testing, after all, seeks to deny autonomy through a widespread surveillance program based on the analysis of people's urine. It is hard to imagine a policy that could more directly confront long-held values in this area.

The other key dimensions of the legal attack on testing fall under the concept of due process of law. Here, in exploring the issues of accuracy and fairness, we see that there is not necessarily as much inherent conflict between these values and the administration of a well-run drug-testing program.

Due Process: Accuracy and Fairness

> I think that the opportunity [for those controlling and administering these tests] to abuse this thing is too great. It could turn into a way to get rid of someone unjustifiably.
>
> —Craftsman, age 35 (625)

While the majority of those workers opposed to testing based their opposition on privacy claims, many cited concerns that fall more directly under the scope of due process of law. Through the application of the Fifth and Fourteenth Amendments to the Constitution, due process protections—including those of the Fourth Amendment—have been broadened and extended to a variety of institutional sites and practices in recent decades (Abraham 1988).[8]

Due process covers far too many things to address here, but in general it requires that when the government acts to search, seize, or otherwise affect the liberty or property of the individual, it must follow the rules.

Although it may well be futile to attempt definitive interpretations of "due process of law" it is possible to delineate certain fundamentals. One basic requirement of the concept "due process of law" is that government may not act in an "arbitrary," "capricious," or "unreasonable" manner in performing its tasks vis-a-vis the body politic. (Abraham 1988, 93)

The decisions of the Warren Court that extended and enforced due process standards in law enforcement are controversial to say the least. It has been argued that due process standards are responsible for freeing vast numbers of criminals, have made the system of law enforcement a mockery, and have been responsible for rising crime rates for the last three decades.[9] But due process, thought to be the protector of criminals and the bane of law enforcers, plays a much more complex role in the drug-testing cases. Indeed, due process arguments seem to advance the social control program manifest in drug testing.

How is this so? As Abraham explains, due process of law holds that government actions should not be performed in an arbitrary, capricious, or unreasonable manner. In drug-testing cases, this mandate takes two basic forms:

1. Testing procedures should make every effort to ensure accuracy.
2. Those tested should not be chosen through the whim or prejudice of a workplace supervisor.

Accuracy

No drug testing is 100% sure.
                                                —Craftsman, age 31 (244)

Any test conducted by humans is fallible and therefore not reliable!
                                                —Craftsman, age unknown (215)

I don't like the idea of taking aspirin and coming up positive and then either being fired or having to defend yourself for no good reason.
                                                —Craftsman, age 43 (360)

As seen in chapter 4, concerns over accuracy are not as important as concerns over privacy rights but are still a central component in the opposition to drug testing. Fully 63 percent of the workers felt that tests were likely to make mistakes, and 28 percent of those who opposed testing cited the accuracy problem in an open-ended query. Accuracy, through due process provisions, has also been at the center of a number of court decisions. As with other areas of this controversy, there has been much disagreement among judges. Most agree that the EMIT test is too subject to error to be solely relied on as an indicator of drug use. The proportion of false positives—false accusations—ranges anywhere from 7 to 38 percent, depending on the study cited (Morgan 1987).

As the district court in *Jones v. McKenzie*[10] concluded after reviewing a number of critiques of the EMIT tests,

> On the basis of the undisputed facts and these persuasive authorities, plaintiff is entitled to a summary judgment that her termination on the basis of a single unconfirmed EMIT test was arbitrary and capricious. (628 F. Supp. at 1506)

The courts are more divided over whether or not testing programs are accurate enough to satisfy due process requirements when a second-stage confirmation test follows the use of an EMIT test. Under the typical government program, EMITs are used to do a preliminary check on the sample, and any positive results are subject to more sophisticated and costly forms of analysis for confirmation. (Such costly safeguards rarely exist for job applicants and are also not used in many nonunionized private sector workplaces.) Ideally, this confirmation is done using the gold standard of testing, GC/MS analysis. GC/MS analysis is very accurate when used by careful, well-trained, error-proof technicians; when samples are subject to temperature-controlled storage and transportation; when equipment is thoroughly cleaned between each analysis; and when labeling and handling are perfected to avoid mix-ups (Morgan 1988).

Some authorities and judges center on the possibility of mistakes and, despite extensive procedural safeguards, refuse to declare the system accurate enough to put concerns over fairness to rest. The district court in *National Treasury Employees Union v. von Raab* took the strongest stand that I have encountered on the accuracy problem. Judge Collins cited testimony by Dr. Arthur McBay that argued,

> All drug-testing procedures result in false positives. The reliability of all drug determinations, whether by immunoassay or GC/MS, depend on such factors as the certainty of specimen identification; specimen storage, handling and preparation; proper cleaning and calibration of testing instruments and hardware; and the qualification and training of laboratory personnel performing the test and interpreting the results. (649 F. Supp. at 390)

He then concluded that "the drug-testing program is so fraught with dangers of false positive readings as to deny the Customs workers due process of law" (649 F. Supp. at 390). The circuit court, however, vacated his decision and joined the Third Circuit and the Supreme Court in ruling

> The drug-testing program is not so unreliable as to violate due process of law. While the initial screening test, EMIT, may have too high a rate of false-positive results for the presence of drugs, the union does not dispute the evidence that the follow-up test, GC/MS, is almost always accurate, assuming proper storage, handling, and measurement techniques. Customs also employs an elaborate chain of custody procedures to minimize the possibility of false positive readings. Moreover, the employee may resubmit a specimen pronounced positive to a laboratory of his own choosing for retesting. Finally, the Customs Service program includes a quality-assurance feature. Control samples will be intermingled with those of the employees to measure the incidence of false-positive results. (816 F.2d at 182–83, see also *Rushton v. Nebraska Public Power Dist.*, 653 F. Supp. at 1525)

This program is representative of the best that can be offered in attempting to improve the accuracy of testing programs. It is certainly not representative of the national standard, since few private sector firms are willing to pay the price of maintaining such a costly system and, further, there are not enough fully qualified laboratories to support the recent surge in drug testing (*Los Angeles Times*, October 27,

1986). For a number of the scientific authorities involved in this controversy, even this model program would violate due process because of the ongoing factor of human error. However, few judges have dwelled on the accuracy issue; by the late 1980s, federally operated or mandated programs followed the strict guidelines set down in the Mandatory Guidelines for Federal Workplace Drug Testing Programs (53 Fed. Reg. 11969–89, 1988),[11] and these have been accepted as effectively flawless (see Zimmer and Jacobs 1992).

Fairness

To many judges, due process demands are best met when citizens are not searched unless authorities can provide probable cause or at least articulable suspicion that an individual is engaged in wrongdoing. For this reason, drug-testing programs that lack a requirement of individualized suspicion were normally rejected by federal judges. As the district court in *von Raab* ruled, "This dragnet approach, a large scale program of searches and seizures made without probable cause or even reasonable suspicion, is repugnant to the United States Constitution" (649 F. Supp. at 387).

But another way of reading this issue asserts that due process demands are *better* served by suspicionless testing because these programs remove the elements of arbitrariness or discretion from the process of selecting those to be searched. As the Third Circuit stated in *Shoemaker v. Handel,*

> Random searches and seizures that have been held to violate the Fourth Amendment have left the exercise of discretion as to selected targets in the hands of a field officer with no limiting guidelines.[12] In the present case the urine tests are mandated by the administrative scheme. The State Steward has no discretion in conducting the tests. Moreover the State Steward has no discretion as to who will be selected for urine testing. That choice is made by a lottery. . . . Thus we hold that daily selection by lot of jockeys to be subjected to urine testing does not violate the fourth amendment. (795 F.2d at 1143, citations omitted)

Indeed, where many have argued that random testing violates due process and the Fourth Amendment because there is no suspicion, these judges assert that it may be all the better that there is no suspicion. As the district court in *Shoemaker* phrased it,

> There is considerable evidence that a testing approach which requires some element of individualized suspicion would actually *increase* the ability of the steward to act in an arbitrary and unreasonable manner by enabling him to select jockeys for testing without any clearly defined and objective behavioral criteria for detecting impairment. Given that jockeys often would be singled out for testing as a result of their behavioral manifestations, this testing procedure would prove considerably more adversarial and subject to abuse over the long term. (619 F. Supp. at 1103)

If discretion and arbitrariness are the gravamens of due process concerns over the selection of those to be searched, random and postaccident testing serve to overcome the problem. In this way, legal standards having to do with fairness in the application of the law can be made to support the implementation of randomly or universally administered surveillance programs. Legal arguments about probable cause and reasonable suspicion—seen by many to be the center of the privacy protection in the Fourth Amendment— are not just sidetracked. They are inverted to support suspicionless testing. Just as the near elimination of concerns about accuracy works to support testing programs, the fairness prong of due process challenges comes around to support the wider deployment of the suspicionless search.

Watershed Cases: The Supreme Court Rulings

In the late 1980s, the Supreme Court moved to resolve some of the disagreement and confusion seen in the federal court decisions on employee drug testing. Its proclivities were first made apparent when it refused to accept a request for certiorari on a Third Circuit opinion approving random drug testing of racehorse jockeys (*Shoemaker v. Handel*). Then, in the 1988 term, the Supreme Court accepted and ruled on drug-testing programs in the railroad industry and the Customs Service. It was here that the Rehnquist court most clearly laid down its law on employee drug testing.

The following pages explain the Supreme Court majority's position on some of the most important controversies raised by litigants challenging or supporting drug-testing programs in *Skinner v. Railway Labor Executives' Association* and *National Treasury Employees Union v. von Raab*. In these cases, the Supreme Court majority—with strong dissents from Marshall and Brennan and, in *von Raab*, Scalia—ruled that suspicionless drug testing programs do not violate the rights of workers. In taking such a position, the Court rejected the majority of lower federal court decisions that had "invalidated testing schemes where the test was not premised upon individualized suspicion" (see Cornish 1988, 118).

As discussed in chapter 3, surveillance is increasingly used as we move toward a disciplinary approach to social control, and suspicionless drug-testing programs can be seen as one example of this pattern. The alternative juridical approach, it will be recalled, is marked by a limited state in a contractual relation with citizens; systems of surveillance and control are partial and limited by a network of legal rights claims. As already seen, workers who oppose disciplinary programs such as drug testing do so by claiming that they have rights that protect them from such things. In short, as expected, the resistance to discipline finds expression in the appeal to the language of juridical rights.

Assessing the conflict between rights claims and disciplinary forms of social control in the Supreme Court cases at hand, it will be argued that the positions the Court majority takes undermine the legal foundation of oppositional claims. While the minority's dissent voices the logic of the limited state and individual rights, the majority moves away from this view. It does so not just by minimizing privacy concerns but by relying on a version of due process and a logic of social control that actively support the goals and assumptions of disciplinary techniques and administrative control.

While the majority's opinions use juridical terms such as *warranted, reasonable, due process,* and *right*, the deeper logic of the language and decisions comes from a disciplinary approach. If the views put forth in these decisions take hold, then it may be that the language of rights remains but that it has been grafted onto an effectively disciplinary organization of control. If rights have helped citizens control the state, in this context the roles are reversed; they help the state control the citizens.

Skinner and *von Raab*

Skinner v. Railway Labor Executives' Association involved the appeal of
a successful challenge to the FRA's program mandating the testing
of the blood and urine of rail personnel involved in serious accidents.
The program also authorized testing on the basis of reasonable suspicion or after a violation of rules of operation related to safety concerns. *National Treasury Employees Union v. von Raab* was a challenge
to the Customs Service's program calling for the mandatory urine
testing of any employee seeking promotion or transfer to a position
involving that employee with illegal drug trafficking, firearms, or
classified material.

   Almost every imaginable group filed amici curiae in these
cases—from the ACLU to Amtrak, from the AFL-CIO to the Organization of Aircraft Owners and Pilots. These cases received great attention in the press and were closely watched by labor leaders whom
I interviewed. As one of the latter put it when asked how the decision
went, "We lost." Bush attorney general, Richard Thornburgh, on the
other hand, bragged that the decisions had given a "green light" to
the wider use of drug testing.

   These programs were most controversial for testing workers
when there was no suspicion of drug use. In *Skinner* whole train
crews were tested after accidents or rules violations, and in *von Raab*
anyone seeking promotion or transfer to a covered position was
tested. As explained earlier, a requirement of individual suspicion is
an essential part of the privacy protection scheme of the Fourth
Amendment, and the absence of the requirement is essential to the
use of ongoing surveillance techniques. For our purposes here—and
for many of the actual participants—that is the pivotal question in
these cases. Additionally, however, the labor organizations, the
ACLU, and other parties saw these cases as tests for a range of
antitesting arguments based on the values of privacy and due process. Therefore, these cases represent an important test of the Supreme Court's response to the privacy and due process claims made
by the workers in chapter 4 and recognized by some judges. In both
cases the Supreme Court upheld the use of the tests.[13]

   Skinner was the case in which the majority and dissenting opinions most thoroughly addressed the issues and laid out their arguments on testing; therefore, it will be the center of attention in the

analysis that follows. In some ways, however, *von Raab* may have a more far-reaching impact since it approves suspicionless testing for employees in a workplace that has—unlike the railroad industry—no apparent history of a drug or alcohol problem. For this reason, Justice Scalia, who supported testing in *Skinner*, dissented in *von Raab*, calling the program "a kind of immolation of privacy and human dignity in symbolic opposition to drug use" (489 U.S. at 681).

The critique that follows argues that the Court's approval of the tests was based on doctrinally and scientifically anomalous positions on a number of key points. Following this, it will be argued that the Court's stance on (1) the reach of the administrative search exception, (2) the basic function of the search, (3) the need for individualized suspicion, and (4) the purpose of a search warrant can be seen as judicial accommodations to the extension of disciplinary forms of social control.[14]

The High Court's Ruling

Safety is the reason that most pro-testing workers give for supporting testing, and it is the topic that opens Justice Kennedy's opinion in *Skinner v. Railway Labor Executives' Association*. He begins by citing FRA studies showing drugs and alcohol to be a contributing factor to a number of railway accidents and fatalities in the 1970s and early 1980s. (As seen in chapter 3, the FRA's more recent postaccident testing program disputes the findings of these early studies.) The next step is to explain the FRA testing program that had been challenged:

> After occurrence of an event which activates its duty to test, the railroad must transport all crew members and other covered employees directly involved in the accident or incident to an independent medical facility, where both blood and urine samples must be obtained from each employee. After the samples have been collected, the railroad is required to ship them by prepaid air freight to the FRA laboratory for analysis. There, the samples are analyzed using "state-of-the-art equipment and techniques" to detect and measure alcohol and drugs. (*Skinner,* 489 U.S. at 609–10).

In *National Treasury Employees Union v. von Raab*, there was no history of drug-related accidents or corruption. Indeed, William von Raab, the commissioner of the Customs Service, is quoted in the Court's opinion as stating that "Customs is largely drug-free" (489 U.S. at 660). Nonetheless, "in May 1986, the Commissioner announced implementation of the drug-testing program" covering those seeking transfer to or employment in jobs involving them in drug law enforcement, requiring them to carry a weapon, or giving access to classified material (489 U.S. at 660).

> After an employee qualifies for a position . . . the Service advises him by letter that his final selection is contingent upon successful completion of drug screening. An independent contractor contacts the employee to fix the time and place for collecting the sample. On reporting for the test, the employee must produce photographic identification and remove any outer garments, such as a coat or a jacket, and personal belongings. The employee may produce the sample behind a partition, or in the privacy of a bathroom stall if he so chooses. To ensure against adulteration of the specimen, or substitution of a sample from another person, a monitor of the same sex as the employee remains close at hand to listen for the normal sounds of urination. Dye is added to the toilet water to prevent the employee from using the water to adulterate the sample. (489 U.S. at 661)[15]

After the specimen is checked for proper color and temperature, it is marked, signed, and submitted to a laboratory.

In each case, after reviewing the contradictory rulings of the district and circuit courts, Kennedy presents his own analysis of the Fourth Amendment issues at stake.[16] As explained earlier, the central questions after the Fourth Amendment has been brought to bear center on whether the search is a "reasonable" one. Justices Marshall and Brennan dissented from the majority by arguing that a search is per se unreasonable unless based on a warrant, probable cause, or at the least reasonable individualized suspicion. They argue, inter alia, that a requirement of individual suspicion would protect individual privacy while not impairing the state interest in safety and drug control and should remain in force (489 U.S. at 641–50).

Justice Kennedy's majority opinions, however, note that the

Fourth Amendment does not prohibit searches, only unreasonable ones. In *Skinner*, he quotes the Fourth Amendment but stops after the first clause to avoid citing the amendment's reference to probable cause or the warrant requirement (489 U.S. at 613). What Kennedy chooses to omit—the standard of individualized suspicion—is also absent from the definition of the reasonable search that is developed in his opinion. Indeed, after citing precedents that were, with one exception, created within the five preceding years, Kennedy notes that *Skinner* "reaffirms the longstanding principle that neither a warrant nor probable cause, nor indeed, any measure of individualized suspicion, is an indispensable component of reasonableness in every circumstance" (489 U.S. at 665).

While that may be true for some types of searches, it must be emphasized that a search as intrusive as body fluid drug testing had never come close to being allowed in the absence of suspicion. This issue had been widely discussed in the law reviews. James had concluded that allowing urinalysis in the absence of suspicion was "not a logical outgrowth of American jurisprudence" (1988, 137).[17] Miller (1986), after a review of the emerging judicial stance on testing programs, concludes that *Shoemaker v. Handel*, one of the earliest cases to allow suspicionless testing, could only be explained as an "anomaly." And it was clear that the majority of lower courts saw suspicionless testing as unconstitutional. Indeed, as seen earlier, the district court in *von Raab* had called such programs "dragnet" searches and declared them "repugnant" to the constitution (649 F. Supp. at 386).

In the majority opinions, however, the Supreme Court allows what they define as a state-action search of a large group of people in the absence of any degree of probable cause or even reasonable suspicion. While earlier cases have carved out numerous exceptions to Fourth Amendment restrictions, this appears to be the first time that the Court has approved such a search for civilians (see *Skinner*, 489 U.S. at 640, Marshall, J., dissenting).

To make the case for a warrantless search, Kennedy argues that the tests are meant to serve administrative "special needs" of the government rather than needs related to criminal law enforcement. That done, Kennedy evaluates the reasonableness of the program by balancing government and individual interests. He argues that the tests are not overly intrusive or violative of privacy expectations and that the government interests outweigh what minimal objections may exist.[18]

Administrative License

In effect, the courts have carved out an exception to traditional Fourth Amendment constraints that would allow what have been variously described as "regulatory searches," "administrative searches," or "inspections." (The original precedent involved granting government inspectors the power to examine residential and commercial buildings for possible violations of health, safety, and sanitary standards.) The essence of this exception is that searches not conducted as part of a typical police investigation to secure criminal evidence but as part of a "general regulatory scheme"—one applying standardized procedures to minimize the potential for arbitrariness—need not be based on individualized suspicion. (Kamisar 1987, 113)

Under the standards of administrative searches, if the government has a compelling "special need" to engage in noncriminal searches of traditionally regulated sites, some standards relating to criminal searches may be relaxed. Initially, a search had to satisfy several threshold requirements before it could be assigned to this exceptional category. Throughout the 1980s, however, standards have been loosened or abandoned to the point where the court may merely declare that the search meets "special needs, beyond the normal need for law enforcement" (*New Jersey v. T.L.O.*, 469 U.S. at 351, Blackmun, J., concurring; see Schulhofer 1989).

The old standards, developed in *Camara v. Municipal Court*, included the following demands. First, there must be a long history of judicial and public acceptance of the program of enforcement. Second, there must be a strong public interest in the search due to the lack of alternatives. And, third, the search must be a limited invasion of individual privacy in the form of a nonpersonal, noncriminal search (James 1986, 134; Schulhofer 1989; see *Camara*, 387 U.S. at 523; *Railway Labor Executives' Association v. Burnley*, 839 F.2d at 586). By these standards, the drug-testing programs before the Court would surely fail.

On the first point, as James (1988) has argued, it is problematic to hold that there is a long history of "public and judicial" acceptance behind the urine testing of unsuspected persons. The policies are both new and strongly opposed in a number of sectors—including at least a few chambers in the districts and circuits of the federal judiciary.

The second point relates to the persuasiveness of the government's interest in safety. The rub here is that a number of lower courts have concluded that because drug tests cannot measure current impairment, there is not a reasonable nexus between the stated job safety concerns and the broad scope of the tests. In other words, since the safety risk of on-the-job impairment is the stated concern of the government and since urinalysis fails to show this condition, the original concern and the testing policy are not reasonably related to each other.[19]

On the third point, previous Supreme Court decisions on administrative searches had only allowed searches in the absence of reasonable suspicion if they were minimally intrusive and noncriminal ones such as the check of an automobile at an international border (see Kamisar 1987).[20] In dealing with this potential problem, Justice Kennedy—as seen more fully below—portrayed drug tests as minimally intrusive and argued that railroad employees' "expectations of privacy . . . are diminished by reason of their participation in an industry that is regulated pervasively to ensure safety" (*Skinner*, 489 U.S. at 627).

In the case of *Skinner*, though not *National Treasury Employees Union v. von Raab*, there is an even more basic problem with using the administrative exception; as Marshall points out, the program regulations state that other parties and litigants will have access to urine samples. Since these other parties would include law enforcement agencies, he argues that the searches are effectively criminal rather than administrative and that they therefore face the stricter Fourth Amendment requirements relating to criminal searches.[21]

Judges determining whether the administrative search exception applies to employee drug testing had fallen all over the board prior to Kennedy's ruling. Indeed, the circuit court in *Lovvorn v. City of Chattanooga* ruled,

> Given the origins of the administrative search warrant exception, it seems incredible that the arguments in favor of mandatory drug testing should be based on this argument. (846 F.2d at 1546)

Kennedy accomplished the incredible by using the more relaxed concept of "special needs" to replace the demanding *Camara* test (Schulhofer 1989, 104). During the 1980s, the Supreme Court was enthusiastic in its use and support of the administrative search exception. It allowed random police checks of automobile disassemblers (*New York v. Burger*), searches of a probationers' home without probable cause of a violation (*Griffin v. Wisconsin*), a search of a government worker's desk without probable cause (*O'Connor v. Ortega*), and the search of a public school student's purse without probable cause (*New Jersey v. T.L.O.*).

It was this last case that has been widely seen as a watershed, and it is here that the elastic language of special needs emerged in a concurrence by Justice Blackmun. In deciding whether administrative standards apply, Blackmun said the court must find "special needs, beyond the normal need for law enforcement [that] make the warrant and probable cause requirements impracticable" before it could "substitute its balancing of interests for that of the Framers" (*T.L.O.*, 469 U.S. at 351).

Tipping the Balance

Once drug-testing programs have been classified as administrative searches involving "special needs" of the government, judges typically, but not universally, discard the idea of search warrants or probable cause in judging the validity of a search. What they turn to instead is what they depict as a balancing of the privacy concerns of workers against the state interest in conducting the search. If the privacy interests of workers are felt to outweigh the needs of the government, then the search is unreasonable. If, on the other and more prevalent hand, the needs of the state outweigh the rights of the individual, then a search—even one lacking any modicum of individualized suspicion—is reasonable.

The beginning point for the balancing maneuver in Fourth Amendment "special needs" decisions is often a citation of *Bell v. Wolfish*, in which the Supreme Court ruled,

The test of reasonableness under the Fourth Amendment is not capable of precise definition or mechanical application. In each case it requires a balancing of the need for the particular search against the invasion of personal rights that the search entails. Courts must consider the scope of the particular intrusion, the manner in which it is conducted, the justification for initiating it and the place in which it is conducted. (441 U.S. at 559)

The pattern of judicial decisions on drug testing certainly endorses the first sentence of the preceding quotation. In performing a balancing act, judges must decide how great an invasion a particular urine-testing program represents and how great the state interest in invading that privacy is. Additionally, they must decide how great an expectation of privacy—if any—a particular class of employees possesses. Obviously, such things are neither quantifiable nor even commensurable in any sense of these terms; balancing adds nothing more than a patina of pseudoeconomistic cost-benefit analysis to a judicial opinion (see also Shapiro 1966).[22] In the cases at hand, Kennedy establishes a framework of assumptions and goals that easily tilts the balance toward the government's surveillance program.

The State Interest

The crux of the "state interest" in *Skinner v. Railway Labor Executives' Association* is safety on the rails. Kennedy's decision opened with a listing of the damage, death, and injury caused by rail accidents in which it was believed that drugs or alcohol were contributing factors. In response to this history, the FRA had imposed the testing regulations. In Kennedy's view, the testing program would reduce or eliminate these types of accidents; therefore, the government had a very weighty interest in pursuing the policy at stake. His portrait can be disputed on a number of points. As seen earlier, recent studies by the FRA have shown that the drug and alcohol role in accidents was less than initially believed. Such findings should reduce the sense of crisis that dominated the Court's assessment of the government interest in rail safety.

But the main problem appears to rest with the efficacy of testing. It is well known that urine tests do not provide information about whether a person is currently under the influence or when and how much of a drug was used. In short, they may tell us that a person used drugs but not whether they were under the influence on the hour, day, or even week that the accident occurred; they say nothing about the cause of the accident. Recognizing that, Kennedy argues that a government search is suitably important if it has "any tendency to make the existence of any fact that is of consequence to the determination (of the point in issue) more or less probable than it would be without the evidence" (489 U.S. at 632). Needless to say, this is a less than stringent scrutiny of the policy at hand.

Another, and I think dispositive, aspect of the state's interest is deterrence (489 U.S. at 632). As explained more fully below, Kennedy argues that the effectively dense pattern of surveillance represented by the ongoing threat of a postaccident test will deter train crews from using drugs at all.[23]

The Privacy Claim

Claims that testing violates privacy are the critical counterpoint to the state interest in the Court's balancing game; the greater the perceived violation of privacy, the more difficulty there is in justifying the search. Justice Scalia was firm in his dissent to *National Treasury Employees Union v. von Raab*, where he found it "obvious that [drug testing] is a type of search particularly destructive of privacy and offensive to personal dignity" (489 U.S. at 680).[24]

But in *Skinner v. Railway Labor Executives' Association* Justice Kennedy was more ambivalent, writing at one point, "[I]t is clear that the collection and testing of urine intrudes upon expectations of privacy that society has long recognized as reasonable" (489 U.S. at 617), and at another, seven pages later, "By and large, intrusions on privacy under the FRA regulations are limited."

As seen above, a number of federal judges have ruled that urine tests are highly intrusive on the grounds that they involve a traditionally private and culturally sensitive activity, that analysis can reveal a wide body of information about the subject, and that the search provides information on activity that may have occurred more than a month before. Despite the weight of judicial and academic opinion in this area, Kennedy dispatches these concerns with a few brief paragraphs (489 U.S. at 624–25).

The Supreme Court majority argues the urine tests are not unacceptably invasive of privacy because they "are not invasive of the body," are collected in a medical environment, and are administered to people who have a "diminished" expectation of privacy due to their participation in a pervasively regulated industry.

Kennedy begins by noting that urine tests, like breath tests, are not all that intrusive because they are not actually invasive of the body. The argument holds that unlike blood, the fluid in question regularly emanates from the body regardless of whether the government is compelling urination and seizing the fruits of the process. Numerous other judges have ruled that while urine does regularly emanate, it is not normally seized and analyzed by government or corporate authorities. Therefore, they argue, urine tests are equivalent to other intrusive body fluid searches. In this matter of legal disagreement, the Court, as with other disputed issues in this case, stands on the side of the surveillance program.

Almost no court has completed an analysis of the privacy impact of urine testing without encountering the concerns raised by the involvement of bodily exposure and urination. To relieve any discomfort with this aspect of drug-testing programs, Kennedy makes two points. His first one is based on the contested position that no one actually watches closely as the urine is passed into the cup. Marshall disputes this by pointing out that the Field Manual distributed by the FRA does actually call for visual monitoring as an assurance that samples are not substituted or tampered with.[25]

As the manual instructs,

The employee will take a urine collection cup into a private area designated by the physician/technician (a restroom or examining room is preferred). *Under direct observation* by the physician/technician, the employee will provide a urine specimen into a polystyrene cup. Employees must provide at least 60 milliliters of urine. Failure to provide a sufficient amount of urine may result in disciplinary action. (FRA Field Manual D-5 [1986], emphasis in original)

Kennedy relies on another version of the regulations that states that visual monitoring is strongly preferred but not necessary. Assuming that visual monitoring does not occur, he then argues that the aural monitoring in which the state agent "listens for the sounds of normal urination" is sufficiently less intrusive to mitigate concerns in this area.

Kennedy also argues that the urine is collected in a "medical environment . . . and thus is not unlike similar procedures encountered in the context of regular physical examination" (489 U.S. at 626–27). In short, the fact that a function performed in a doctor's office is similar to a function performed by a state investigator has mitigated concern over the state's action.[26] One must wonder if a state-ordered blood or urine test under the suspicion of culpable malfeasance is not somewhat less routine than a blood or urine test in a medical office. But what is perhaps more interesting is the implication that what is sanctioned by medical use is equally acceptable when used by the state. Doctors and related personnel are seen as technicians of the human body, and one is apparently allowed no shame or dignity before them.[27]

Finally, Kennedy argues that since railroads have been heavily regulated and many companies require physical exams, rail workers have a diminished expectation of privacy. It may seem odd to make this claim about the subjective state of the workers since they had, in fact, brought this suit arguing that their expectations of privacy had been violated. Another problem with such an argument was raised in the Ninth Circuit's opinion in the railroad testing case.

There is no question that the railroad industry has experienced a long history of close regulation. This regulation has diminished the *owners'* and *managers'* expectations of privacy in railroad premises, but we do not believe it has diminished the individual railroad *employee's* expectation of privacy in his person or body fluids. (*Railway Labor Executives' Association v. Burnley*, 839 F.2d at 585)

Thus we see Kennedy's balance. On one side the Court places the broad social interest in public safety and the government's efforts to control drugs. On the other side we see the apparently less compelling individual employee's interest in avoiding a simple medical check for evidence of illegal drug use.

It is hardly surprising which way the scale tips. But alternative frames for the balancing game exist. For example, one might pit a government agency's interest in using a flawed method of dealing with potential drug use against a free society's attempt to preserve what Brandeis called "the right to be let alone—the most comprehensive of rights and the right most valued by civilized men" (*Olmstead v. United States*, Brandeis, J., dissenting; see also *Capua v. City of Plainfield*).

Another, more precise and appropriate balance would not weigh the privacy intrusion against the gross interest in safety but against the net difference between the promotion of safety under suspicionless testing and the promotion of safety under alternative and less intrusive programs. What should be measured, in short, is not the overall interest in increasing safety, but the potential marginal gain in safety achieved by using suspicionless testing over other policies. By falsely casting suspicionless testing as carrying the whole weight of the state interest, Kennedy sets a balance that has a preordained tilt.

The use of balancing as a replacement for individual suspicion in judging the reasonableness of a search emerged in a series of cases involving what the majorities called "special needs" that were "beyond the normal needs of law enforcement." At first these special needs involved such contexts as prisons, probation programs, and schools, but they have now been expanded to include many government workplaces. Stanley Cohen has argued that the contemporary movement in social control policy expands control mechanisms into new and less punitive sites such as schools and workplaces. As this expansion occurs, a greater part of the population is encompassed by the state's means of surveillance and regulation. In this light, it may be all the more important that protections such as the Fourth Amendment are rigorously applied to these noncriminal settings. But the Court here continues a trend that both encourages the diffusion of control and further relaxes individual rights in the institutional settings to which the means of control are spreading.

Two Modes of Social Control

It should be clear by now that Kennedy's opinion rests on a number of arguments that are strongly disputed within the legal community. Often, such conflicts are the result of fundamentally different ways of approaching and studying a problem or situation. Here, the conflict appears to be between competing analytical frameworks on the questions of rights and social control: the juridically derived rights claims of antitesting workers are faced off against the disciplinary approach to social control seen in both drug-testing programs and the decision of the Court. While Kennedy's tendencies to downplay privacy rights, to "medicalize" social control (Roman 1980), and to fuse administrative and criminal regions of the law all indicate a disciplinary bent, a stronger case is made by taking a close look at the premises, goals, and language of the Court's opinions. Therefore, the pages that follow offer a more thorough analysis of how Kennedy's opinion reflects the elements of disciplinary social control. Further, it will be suggested that Marshall's dissent, which is largely sympathetic to the arguments of those who oppose testing, displays the characteristics of a more juridical framework.

Why Search?

The tensions between juridical and disciplinary approaches are revealed in a number of areas but perhaps most clearly in the rationales behind the competing perspectives on the original justification for the search at hand. In these cases, the professed reasons for drug testing are improving the safety on railroads and ensuring the integrity of customs agents. Additionally, government officials and drug-test sales representatives argue that testing programs improve productivity, reduce absenteeism, and support law enforcement efforts. More important here, however, is the question of how the tests effect these ends.

From one point of analysis, drug tests assist an investigation by confirming or disconfirming the suspicion that an individual has actually used drugs. But from another approach, they enhance a disciplinary effect by setting up a systematic means of observation such that workers know they are being watched and are quite likely to be detected if drugs are used. These approaches may run together in some manners, but the logic behind the positions reveals fundamentally different orientations to the project of social control.

In the first, or juridical perspective, there is a reactive system of law enforcement that activates itself once a violation has occurred and then applies the powers of investigation in an attempt to bring violators to their just deserts. From the second, or disciplinary perspective, the state is an ever-present steward that, by creating an ongoing and systematic structure of surveillance, can greatly reduce the possibility and likelihood of infractions even occurring.

Individual Suspicion and the General Search

This difference is readily apparent in the justices' approaches to the all-important question of individual suspicion. As noted earlier, individual suspicion requirements are an important protector of individual privacy because they require the state to have articulable suspicions of wrongdoing before it may search. This perspective was used by both Marshall in *Skinner v. Railway Labor Executives' Association* and the lower court in *Railway Labor Executives' Association v. Burnley* to decide that reasonable suspicion of an individual was required for drug testing. They argued that a requirement of suspicion would "ensure that the tests are confined to the detection of current impairment, rather than to the discovery of 'the metabolites of various drugs which are not evidence of current intoxication and may remain in the body for days or weeks after the ingestion of the drug'" (*Skinner*, 489 U.S. at 613, quoting lower court opinion).

With a requirement of individual suspicion, criminal authorities—unless due to luck or a tip—go to work in the wake of criminal activity, and their primary function is to investigate the crime and bring individual wrongdoers to justice. The relationship between the state and the population at large is more limited and represents a less efficient economy of power under this model; criminals may be less subject to state intervention, but so are more well-behaved common citizens or those on the borderline (see Cohen 1979).

But the logic of Kennedy's justification is different. As he concludes,

By ensuring that employees in safety-sensitive positions know they will be tested upon the occurrence of a triggering event, the timing of which no employee can predict with certainty, the regulations significantly increase the deterrent effect of the administrative penalties associated with the prohibited conduct. (*Skinner*, 489 U.S. at 630)[28]

The logic behind this search is not one of crime and investigation; indeed, Kennedy explicitly argues that traditional, low-surveillance crime and punishment policies do not work (*Skinner*, 489 U.S. at 629–30). The purpose of the program is to establish an ongoing precrime search that will work against even the possibility of misbehavior.

The Unwarranted Warrant

The distinction between the juridical and disciplinary approaches is also apparent in the differing views of the search warrant. When Marshall discusses the warrant requirement and other Fourth Amendment protections, they are viewed primarily as a check on unnecessary government intrusion into the lives of individuals (*Skinner v. Railway Labor Executives' Association*, 489 U.S. at 640). His stance is that the warrant provides an assurance that the government has a very good reason before it encroaches on the peace and privacy of the individual. Marshall's definition pushes the issue of probable cause and therefore enforces an individually oriented responsive model of investigation; it conflicts with and would limit the totalizing search because of its emphasis on individual suspicion. As the court in *Capua v. City of Plainfield* stated, "No prohibition more significantly distinguishes our democracy from a totalitarian government than that which bars warrantless searches and seizures" (643 F. Supp. at 1511).

But when Kennedy speaks of the warrant, he marks its purpose as simply ensuring that intrusions are regulated, nondiscretionary, and carefully applied (*Skinner*, 489 U.S. at 621–22). His framing of the warrant, stressing authorization, nondiscretion, and clarity surrounding the purpose of the search, leaves little room to challenge the legality of explicitly defined but preemptive and widespread searches for evidence of misbehavior. Carefully regulated, nondiscretionary searches meet his requirements. Indeed, he concludes that the railway drug-testing plan so totally guarantees all the comforts of a search warrant that "a warrant would do little to further these aims" (*Skinner*, 489 U.S. at 622).

In all these ways, then, the new Fourth Amendment jurisprudence of the Supreme Court accommodates the panoptic search that is central to the disciplinary society.

The Disciplining of Rights

While Michel Foucault thought rights claims would be the likely form of opposition as new forms of disciplinary surveillance techniques were deployed, I think he had little expectation that such a form of opposition would work. This is because the new techniques carry their own logic, or their own set of rules, which displace or colonize the once noble claims of the juridical system's matrix of rights.

The case of employee drug testing provides a fascinating example of how new techniques of discipline are deployed and legal hurdles overcome. After noting that mechanisms of discipline tended to originate in settings such as prisons or military camps, Foucault argued that they would "have a certain tendency to become 'de-institutionalized', to emerge from the closed fortresses in which they once functioned and to circulate in a 'free' state" (Foucault 1979, 211). Through this expansion, schools, welfare programs, and workplaces become sites for the disciplining of the broader society. This pattern was followed in the case of drug testing as the military undertook the first extensive use and development prior to wider implementation. In a military setting, the use of suspicionless testing received early approval from the courts because the relationship between the soldier and the state is so much different than that between the citizen and the state. As the court ruled in one of the early military drug-testing cases,

> The fundamental necessity for obedience, and the consequent necessity for imposition of discipline, may render permissible within the military that which would be constitutionally impermissible outside of it. (*Committee for GI Rights v. Callaway*, 518 F.2d at 468).

But drug testing quickly spread to workplaces outside the military where we would have expected it to be found, in the judge's words, "constitutionally impermissible." At first, as we have seen, these expectations were realized when both workers who opposed testing and many judges who presided over testing cases concluded that these control techniques were impermissible under our constitutional framework.

But it is also possible that the disciplining of social control could render those legal obstacles harmless, or, in a sense, make the rights claims themselves "impermissible." As James observed in her analysis of a lower court ruling in *von Raab*, which the Supreme Court affirmed,

The standard of review in *von Raab* parallels the acceptable standard of review in the military cases first challenging federal drug testing programs. . . . In the nation's "war on drugs," the federal work place has experienced a "militarization" of its test of reasonableness. (1988, 138–39)

With recent court decisions, suspicionless testing has expanded a significant degree into the free society, and so, apparently, has the "fundamental necessity for obedience." The Supreme Court's "militarization of its test of reasonableness," refashioning of due process, and rejection of the bid for privacy may mean that not just the workers but the rights claims upon which they relied have been brought into the disciplinary fold.

Chapter 6

Conclusion: Legitimating the Gaze

[I]n extending approval of drug testing to that category consisting of employees who carry firearms, the Court exposes vast numbers of public employees to this needless indignity. Logically, of course, if those who carry guns can be treated in this fashion, so can all others whose work, if performed under the influence of drugs, may endanger others—automobile drivers, operators of other potentially dangerous equipment, construction workers, school crossing guards.

Justice Antonin Scalia,
National Treasury Employees Union v. von Raab

While the Supreme Court's decisions applied to a fairly unique set of circumstances, federal court decisions in the wake of *Skinner v. Railway Labor Executives' Association* and *von Raab* have largely confirmed Scalia's fears.[1] Random testing has been approved for government employees who carry a gun, for those involved in drug law enforcement and, in several agencies, for those who simply drive a car.[2] One must wonder, with Justice Scalia, if the logic of *von Raab* means that "a law requiring similar testing of private citizens who use dangerous instruments such as guns or cars . . . would also be constitutional" (*Skinner*, 489 U.S. at 686). As Schulhofer put it, "[R]egulators stand invited to involve other search and surveillance techniques, in the workplace and beyond, under the ever-more permissive administrative search rubric" (1989, 88).

The Supreme Court's ruling discounted and rejected the arguments of workers who opposed drug testing and paved the way for the wider use of testing in the American workplace. By reclassifying largely criminal policies as administrative and colonizing the workplace as a site of surveillance and control, these decisions further "widen the net and thin the mesh" of social control (see Cohen 1985, 42-43). Ongoing surveillance in the absence of any individualized suspicion of wrongdoing is acceptable. Indeed, by the emergent meaning of due process, it may even be more "just" than a search made under individualized suspicion, because the discretionary and corruptible act of identifying suspicious people is eliminated.

The Court's upholding of the suspicionless search may not represent a "logical outgrowth of American jurisprudence" (James 1988, 137). But it is a logical outgrowth of a discourse of social control that must privilege ongoing surveillance and preemptive discipline and thus cannot accommodate a discourse based on limited state observation and retroactive sanction. This logic both signals and advances the further reorganization of social control and individual rights in the United States and points to the creation of such a permanent matrix of observation that the possibility of wrongdoing is almost precluded.

The *language* of rights, which was so important to workers who oppose testing, remains salient in the courts. Judges speak of reasonableness, legitimacy, privacy, due process, and other terms that are reminiscent of the Constitution and the Bill of Rights. But it appears that these words, which are almost infinitely malleable, can often come to mask changes that are sanctioned by the courts but that bear little resemblance to the system of rights that is referred to by workers, legal activists, and others using legal strategies in this policy dispute.

The legal and political struggles over drug testing and related techniques are not over. As lawsuits continue, assessments and policies change, and as new technical twists emerge, new facets of this controversial area will undoubtedly emerge. But for now, it is possible to reach some tentative conclusions about the new law of surveillance that is emerging from the courts' rulings.

The Legitimation of General Surveillance

Legitimate Vision: Testing and Privacy

The most fundamental challenge to testing seen in these struggles was the claim that it violates the right of privacy—the right to be "let alone" (Warren and Brandeis 1890, 195). But American workers are losing the right to be let alone as the courts discount and reject their claims at nearly every turn.

The claim to informational privacy is summed up under the popular saying, It's none of your business. This challenge to surveillance policy met with the assurance that only authorized personnel will have access to information gained through the surveillance program. In *Skinner v. Railway Labor Executives' Association*, this body of personnel can be extended to include law enforcement personnel and litigants in later cases, but this possibility gives the Court only brief pause. As for a simple rejection of the informational intrusion regardless of whether or not it is done by authorized personnel, there has been little, if any, success. Access to information is the indispensable element of successful surveillance: to those workers who say, It's none of your business, the leading courts have said, Yes it is.

The claim to visual privacy and dignity relating to compelled and observed urination has produced a rather odd combination of outcomes. Perhaps most interesting is the suggestion that compelled and observed urination is not bothersome when the agent of authority works in a medical guise. The medical professions have always been linked to disciplinary mechanisms of control, and this outcome clearly confirms that pattern (Cohen 1985; Donzelot 1979; Foucault 1979; Roman 1980).

But another tendency, signaled in *National Treasury Employees Union v. von Raab*, is to simply stop requiring visual observation. While this certainly removes one of the more offensive aspects of the program, it also makes cheating incredibly easy. As Schulhofer (1989) concluded after noting that the program in *von Raab* included several days of advanced warning for testees and no visual observation, it is a very simple matter to either abstain from use or carry in a body flask of clean urine. In adapting this program to fit our cultural sensitivities about "bathroom things," the program was dramatically weakened. Given this, it would seem that the likely tendency in testing programs will be to either stick with directly observed urination or use surprise tests so that employees cannot easily prepare some sort of ruse.

Perfect Vision: Testing Accuracy and the Law

On the question of accuracy, legal challenges have clearly succeeded in improving many drug-testing programs. More accurate confirmation procedures, hearing mechanisms, written regulations, and laboratory certification measures have been worked into almost every program that has passed judicial muster. That does not mean that mistakes will not be made, but it does mean that these well-run programs will have fewer mistakes than will occur under less carefully administered programs. For those workers whose primary concern was accuracy and whose workplace programs have been elevated to the standards of government programs, opposition to testing paid off.

But mistakes were neither the only nor even the primary reason that surveyed workers opposed testing. The opposition was more commonly and powerfully expressed in terms of privacy rights. Privacy arguments, in essence, assert that authorities should not be able to compel urination and analyze body fluids. Accuracy arguments, on the other hand, ask that the surveillance program be competently administered. To bluntly state the difference between the two, the privacy approach says, "Don't do it," while the due process approach says, "Do it well." Due process calls for accuracy are not really opposition to testing—they are a call for better testing.

The pursuit of truth and accuracy is as central to our idea of legal due process as it is to any effective surveillance program. Disciplinary surveillance, like the law, should be foolproof; it should have perfect vision. Therefore, unlike the fundamental conflict between the value of privacy and the implementation of surveillance, due process values can be, and apparently have been, easily embraced within a well-run surveillance program.

Total Vision: Testing and Fairness

The fear of harassment is the other key concern of those who oppose testing programs—that employers and managers will use their discretion in testing to single out and persecute workers who are disliked, who are members of racial minorities, or who create trouble either through union activism or complaints about working conditions. The rights claim mobilized to express this concern is the due process demand that the actions of authorities be fair; that such things as prejudice, personal dislike, or ulterior motivations do not come into play in the administration of regulatory schema.

In the view of many judges, this interest is best met by requiring either a search warrant or at least demonstrable individualized suspicion prior to undertaking a urine test. Under this approach, the demand for fairness also serves as a considerable protector of privacy, because employees will not be subjected to a search unless their employers can demonstrate reasonable grounds of suspicion, such as slurred speech, erratic movements, or the odor of marijuana smoke. Generally, those who avoid such signals are fairly certain to maintain their privacy.

But this rights claim has gone through a redefinition in the Third Circuit and Supreme Court decisions on drug testing. As seen, their decisions have held or implied that the probable cause or suspicion requirement actually threatens the value of fairness because it relies on the discretion of human authorities. Therefore, they argue, random, universal, or postaccident searches are actually more protective of due process claims because they assure that everyone is treated equally.

In short, the search cannot be abused by those in power because everyone is equally subject to the search. In this way, a rights claim that has been closely associated with the protection of privacy is transformed to have an opposite implication—to treat the citizenry fairly, the entire citizenry must be subject to the search. The question of discretion and abuse is addressed not by limiting the search but by totalizing it.

In sum, the courts have overrun or rejected the fundamentally antisurveillance values surrounding the idea of privacy while harnessing due process claims to support general surveillance programs that can assure a relatively high degree of accuracy and a lack of individual harassment.

The Politics of Testing

The social control innovations studied in this book challenge longstanding principles of privacy and due process and subject millions of American workers to degrading, invasive, and generally unnecessary intrusions. Yet most Americans and many of those who would be tested actually support these programs. Those who did not support drug testing mobilized widely respected legal rights to privacy and due process but were largely frustrated. How did this expansion of the surveillance net—which is only part of a broader wave of innovations in control policy—occur with such apparent ease and authority?

As suggested in the opening pages of this book, there is no simple, parsimonious, or fully conclusive answer. But what seems to have taken place is an interplay of forces in the popular culture and the state that created a social, political, and legal context geared to the implementation of this new and innovative technique of control.

Phase One: Generating Consent

The drug crisis campaign that was sponsored by the White House and played out in the mass media clearly served to quell much of the potential opposition to testing and comparable initiatives. Surveyed workers who supported testing often gave a sense of doing it be-grudgingly, one referring to a national crisis and a need for sacrifice on the scale of World War II.[3] One effect of the crisis, then, was to raise fears, redefine expectations, and promote sacrifice and to there-fore curtail political conflict over policy changes. It generated, para-phrasing Gramsci (1985), the "spontaneous consent" of at least some of the masses.

But while the impression of a national drug crisis is an important part of understanding support for testing, it is a mistake to conclude that it can explain the entirety of pro-testing sentiment among work-ers. Indeed, the analysis in chapter 4 suggested that workers' assess-ments of the drug problem in their own workplaces were slightly more important than their perception of national problems in explain-ing their position on testing.

In this light, it is critical to note an important ramification of the distinction between a national drug problem and the situations exist-ing in thousands of different workplaces. While general patterns of workplace drug use were greatly exaggerated in the 1980s, there were clearly some workplaces and workers particularly threatened by on-the-job drug use. If a welder forced to work with an intoxicated partner feels that drug testing will remove this threat from his or her life, it may hardly seem reasonable for the remote scholar to deem this a matter of ideological hegemony.[4] Faced with a bad situation and limited options, people do what they can to cope. We might therefore say that for them this is not a case of ideological hegemony but a case of self-interest or, indeed, self-preservation.

But the creation of situations and the limiting of options do not take place in a vacuum; there may be more subtle forms of domination seen in the way that competing policy options are advanced and treated. As E. E. Schattschneider wrote, "The definition of alternatives is the supreme instrument of power" (1960, 168). Drug testing is only one possible and, as seen in chapters 1 and 3, quite flawed way to improve workplace safety. Union leaders, EAP administrators, and some personnel managers have argued that if workers and supervisors can cooperate in paying attention to on-the-job impairment, then they can provide prevention and treatment programs that are highly effective *and* cognizant of workers' rights claims and about preserving their dignity (American Federation of Labor and Congress of Industrial Organizations [AFL-CIO] 1987; Maltby 1987).

Function testing, for example, is a less invasive, less costly, and more effective alternative to drug testing.[5] On reporting for work, employees operate a brief video game or flight simulator and are gauged for the speed and appropriateness of their responses. These types of tests can identify incompetence whether it is tied to drugs, alcohol, the flu, or a sleepless night and can do so without necessarily invading the private life of the worker. Since they measure impairment itself rather than biological traces related to past states of impairment, function tests are a more direct and effective means to improve safety.

An even more fundamental alternative to things like testing would begin with the recognition that a workplace that does have a significant drug problem is undoubtedly facing a larger problem among its staff. If people are so bored and alienated by their jobs and conditions that drug use truly dominates their daily lives, then perhaps more fundamental changes in the organization of work are needed. Engaging people in challenging work and creative decision making may be a more permanent and promising solution to these problems than compelling them to urinate in a jar.

This is not an essay on how to treat drug abusers. The point is that there are ways to deal with a workplace drug problem that may be more comprehensive and effective than testing. At the very least, there are alternatives to testing that do not bring the full invasion and degradation of urine or blood testing. At best, some alternatives could actually empower workers and involve them in workplace management.

Workers who think that the only or best way to improve safety is by allowing management to establish drug-testing programs have overlooked the shortcomings of testing and the promise of viable alternatives. Whether this outcome occurs because of an overreaction to a so-called drug crisis, because management has been able to present a forced option by limiting policy choices, or because drug testing has been widely billed as a panacea for workplace safety, some workers have chosen a problematic and costly road to safety.

Political and economic leaders in the 1980s got behind the testing initiative and pushed it as *the* appropriate response to drug problems. In doing so, they focused on a real problem in some people's lives while limiting the apparent range of policy responses to ones that they favored (see Hall et al. 1978).[6] The ability to define public problems and shape the choices over policy responses is an immense ideological and communicative power.

Phase Two: Containing the Opposition

The drug crisis may have generated the spontaneous consent of some of the masses, but a good chunk of the masses failed to get on board the testing movement. These workers may have sued, quit, filed grievances, lobbied union leaders or personnel directors, just grumbled, or, for those who used drugs, tried to fool the tests.

The latter can buy or borrow clean urine and load it into a rubber flask that is strapped tightly to the body to avoid visual detection and maintain the temperature of the urine. Then, unless urination is very closely observed, a small tube with a valve can be used to produce a drug free sample. These tactics, along with grumbling and complaining about "Big Brother," are among the "everyday forms of resistance" that otherwise powerless people can use (Scott 1985).

Antitesting workers also took more formal and public actions, and these actions have been the focus of this book. At first glance, workers who reject or discount the impression of a national drug crisis and put forth legal claims to privacy and due process appear to debunk the idea of ideological hegemony. After all, if nearly half of these workers reject a policy advanced by both management and the state and supported by an almost overwhelming propaganda campaign in the mass media, how can anything approximating "the spontaneous consent of the masses" be occurring?

For this part of the "masses," consent is simply not spontaneous. Here subjugation involves a more complex pattern in which the opposition to testing was expressed in the apparently meaningful and effective terms of a legal struggle. Lawsuits were filed, lawyers argued, judges judged, and when it was all said and done, the effort to block testing had largely failed. In short, the legal battle studied here had the effect of containing and overwhelming residual conflict over testing that had not been preempted by the drug crisis in the popular culture.

There are two ways to explain how litigation played to this conclusion. From one perspective, workers made a fundamental error by placing their faith in the law. Since the law is the official language of the state, is authoritatively interpreted by an elite class of state workers called judges, and has consistently helped expand the power of both employers and the government, then workers were suckered if they thought the law could do them any good. From this perspective, legal ideology and action serve as "flypaper" (Rosenberg 1991) because they sap resources and displace alternative interpretations and strategies that do not center on legal rights.

But such arguments discount the extent to which the law has sometimes been a promising and productive means for dominated groups to improve their lot. Law, in short, has not been consistently hopeless. In the areas of racial equality and pay equity (McCann 1994; Scheingold 1989), for example, groups have made significant advances through legal action. Therefore, a better cut on what happened here begins by returning to E. P. Thompson's argument that the law can and sometimes does constrain the action of elites and serve the needs of the less powerful. His argument, seen in chapter 1, merits another look:

> On the one hand, it is true that the law did mediate existent class relations to the advantage of rulers . . . On the other hand, the law mediated these class relations through legal forms which imposed, again and again, inhibitions on the actions of the rulers. . . . And not only were the rulers (indeed, the ruling class as a whole) inhibited by their own rules of law against the exercise of direct unmediated force . . . but they also believed enough in these rules and the accompanying ideological rhetoric, to allow,

in certain limited areas, the law itself to be a genuine forum in which certain kinds of class conflict were fought out. (1975, 264–65)

As an ideology that becomes partially autonomous as it is encoded and passed down from generation to generation, the values and principles of the legal order become tools that can be used by many different groups.

In this case legal claims served as an ideological counterforce to the control initiatives that emerged from the War on Drugs. That is not to say that legal ideology is not a part of some broader cultural hegemony; indeed, many authors see it as the classic example of a hegemonic ideology that reifies and legitimates while allowing a zone of acceptable, if relatively minor, struggle. In terms of the overall maintenance of the state, law is obviously a key element of legitimation and domination (Scheingold 1989).

What has been studied here, however, is one of these relatively minor struggles over the implementation of one particular type of social control mechanism. It has been a small, though significant, adjustment in the relations of power, not a fundamental shift on a Gramscian scale. In such a context, as Thompson's work has shown, legal claims can serve as an effective source of culturally legitimate counterpoints to the claims and initiatives of elites. Thus, legal concepts and principles can be used by nonelites as an empowering means of expression and tactic of action. Whether that happens and works depends, as Thompson emphasizes, on the historical context of political and legal struggles. Thus the rights of privacy and due process *might* have worked to block testing, *if* the times and the judges had been different.

The Times and the Judges

The greatest of all legal fictions is that the law itself evolves, from case to case, by its own impartial logic, true only to its own integrity, unswayed by expedient considerations. (Thompson 1976, 250)

Mythical beliefs about law hold that The Law is or can be a largely fixed and autonomous set of rules or principles (Carter and

Gilliom 1989). This vision of the law discounts the importance of individual judges and the historical contingency of legal rulings. From these perspectives, it is the law, not the judges, that has ruled on these cases, and we should expect a relatively uniform response to the basic issues in testing controversies.

There is uniformity in judicial decisions on drug testing to the extent that judges concur that testing claims involve the Fourth Amendment and privacy and due process concerns. The very fact that participants in these conflicts center on a concept like rights and other elements of legal discourse shows that this language does "push toward uniformity" (Brigham 1984). The significance of this fact should not be understated: A reality that starts out as a potential cacophony ends up being organized into a shared cultural language. In this way, the legal framework serves as a "symbolic framework in terms of which to formulate, think about, and react to political problems" (Geertz 1973; see McCann 1989).

But a common vocabulary does not imply uniform conclusions; on more specific issues, judicial decisions on drug testing have been so diverse and contradictory that it is impossible to discount the importance of differences among individual judges. Judges have opined that urine tests do and do not constitute a search, that they do and do not provide a valid measure of drug use, and that they do and do not significantly violate privacy. Many courts have ruled that due process requirements are violated unless testing is based on some form of individual suspicion, while others have ruled that a requirement of suspicion actually threatens these rights. The concept of privacy itself has experienced numerous definitions with some seeming to imply that the relationship between the citizen and the state is an intimate personal affair. It has even been concluded that the state has a greater interest in regulating the behavior of race horse jockeys than the behavior of police officers and fire fighters. And, of course, we have seen Supreme Court justices start from the same Fourth Amendment and reach antithetical conclusions.[7]

It is at this level of discursive anarchy and political maneuver that winners and losers are selected and public policy is shaped. And it is here that the political goals and ideologies behind judicial appointments take on a great deal of importance. No one can seriously doubt that if the federal courts were solely peopled by Brennans and Marshalls, these bids to oppose testing would have met much greater success. Within the general framework of the law, then, it matters very much who the judges are.

President Reagan agreed with this conclusion and is said to have considered his appointments to the Supreme Court "his most important legacy" (Baum 1989, 40).[8] Prospective justices were carefully screened and underwent lengthy interviews on their judicial and political philosophies (Baum 1989, 41; Goldman 1989, 308). They were chosen, in large part, because of their tough stands on law and order issues and because of their opposition to the expansive view of legal rights that marked the Warren Court. Therefore, when a law and order program such as employee drug testing is opposed by people using Warren era rights claims, it is hardly surprising that antitesting claims lose. They represent all the wrong things to the current majority.

In some of the cases reviewed in chapter 5, antitesting arguments faced anything but rejection; indeed, they were victorious and the judicial opinions were elegant expressions of opposition arguments. But it appears that such judicial responses will be increasingly frustrated by the line of arguments set down by the Supreme Court.[9] The Court's decision not only rejected many central antisurveillance rights claims; it appears to have struck a blow at the very tradition of legal reasoning that produced them. Such a blow could only be expected from justices who were, in large part, selected to strike it.

Postscript

Super Vision: The Rise of the Watchful Eye in Social Control Policy

He knows when you've been sleeping;
He knows when you're awake,
He knows when you've been bad or good,
So be good for goodness sake.
                    —"Santa Claus Is Comin' to Town"

As this seemingly innocent holiday song shows, our culture's myths have long held the threat or promise of a power that is able to see and know all. We envision a force like God, Santa Claus, or Big Brother that is able to cross the boundaries of space, time, even flesh, and be aware of what we have done in our homes, in our past, or with our bodies. But, for a long time, that was all myth; the omniscient authority was a figment of our cultural imagination. Today, this power is becoming a reality in social control policy.

The full explanation for the rise of this new visual power cannot rest solely on the events and actors of the last few years. Indeed, Bentham's visionary descriptions of the panopticon were written in 1787, and the use of increased surveillance to control and modify human behavior has been widespread, if not consistently expanding, since then. Progressives, New Dealers, and the reformers of more recent decades sought to rein in corrupt and dangerous businesses with wider government inspections and audits and greater access to information. The law enforcement community has deployed finger-printing, national data banks, wire and phone taps, bugs, undercover surveillance, and other means of catching criminals through an enhanced ability to see. And the corporate community, using sophisticated marketing research, keeping in-depth records of consumer credit, and targeting potential customers through careful demographic analysis, has also participated in this broadly based movement.

By all accounts, we are at the beginning of a wave of technical advances in the means of surveillance. DNA testing, hair follicle and saliva testing, AIDS testing, computer matching, and other techniques all promise to increase the depth, breadth, and density of the state's ability to survey and control. At the same time, we face an apparent rise in the need to control—social and health sciences increasingly tell us of the interdependency of health, wealth, and well-being in modern society. In short, those of us who don't smoke, don't use drugs, don't drive drunk, don't have AIDS or tuberculosis, don't exceed the speed limit, or don't have genetic illnesses that overload insurance programs, face an increasing motivation and ability to discover and control those who do and thereby threaten us. In this context, claims to rights of privacy and autonomy will be increasingly thrust into the debates of the legislatures and courtrooms. The most disturbing implication of this book, however, is that such claims may become the least useful when they are the most needed, as they are colonized by the demands of the disciplinary state.

Appendixes

Appendix 1

Survey Administration
and Coding

The survey was administered by mail in October, 1989. It was directed to that portion of the union membership employed in work areas most likely to be affected by drug-testing programs—2,167 individuals. Each of these members received a preliminary card informing them that the survey was coming and that it was interesting, important, and easy and would take about five minutes to complete. Enclosed with the survey was a stamped return envelope as well as a brief letter from the manager of the union local requesting their input and ensuring confidentiality but avoiding any statements that might lead respondents one way or another in their views. Given these measures and the interest level in the topic, the response rate was 38 percent. This return rate (819 cases out of a possible 2,167) was stronger than expected and certainly good for this type of survey technique on this type of population.

There are two closely related points to be made about the response rate in this instance. First, the response rate should provide a fairly good measure of who cares enough about this issue to do anything about it; if so, the number that failed to respond represents a high rate of acquiescence. While four to eight minutes is a time commitment, so is voting in either union or public elections, letter writing, petition gathering, or other means of expression. Thus, it may very well be that roughly 60 percent of the union membership is not interested enough in the topic at hand to respond, though other factors might also be involved. Second, there may be somewhat more intense feelings among those who took the time to participate. Therefore, this group may represent a slightly clarified picture of opinions within the membership at large. When encountering the sharp polarization of views on several of the topics in the survey, one should remember that there may have been more moderate or middle-of-the-scale views if a larger response rate had been achieved.

While one might assume that only those interested in drug testing would respond to such a survey, the distribution of results suggests that many of the respondents are more interested in safety and the national drug problem than they are in the specific issue of drug testing. Others may participate because of a general interest in union policy. Therefore, given the variety of motivational incentives to participate, I think concerns over a great degree of systematic bias, though obviously valid, do not endanger the overall usefulness of the survey.

While stressing that this sample is not scientifically representative, I do think that it provides enough individual cases and enough variety of opinions to allow statistical analysis and comparisons of different subgroups within the overall survey group. Many of the statistical measures used assume randomness in sample derivation; while this assumption has not been met in a technical sense, with the large number of cases and multiple reasons for participating in the survey, it is safe to assume that these measures can still provide useful information about the data at hand.

One drawback of a mail survey is that it precludes the opportunity to engage in any form of dialogue with the respondents. Therefore, such things as what someone means by "privacy" or whether someone has good evidence of a safety problem cannot be clarified by asking repeated questions of all subjects. At one level, this is simply a given liability that must be accepted in an effort to learn something about a large population at a feasible rate of expenditure. But such a tendency may have been somewhat mitigated by the fact that very early in the survey, before questions introducing material that may have offered leads or suggestions, we included a question asking,

> Whether you support, oppose or feel neutrally about testing programs, could you briefly tell us why you feel this way? Please write down the one or two main reasons for your views.

A very high nonresponse rate had been expected on this question, but both the number and depth of responses were quite gratifying (although the overall rate of survey participation was undoubtedly reduced). Fully 84 percent of the respondents participated in the open-ended section, and many offered paragraph-length responses or even additional pages of commentary. These responses provide

insight into the expression of views that might be less clear or poig-
nant in an individual's response to a scaled, close-ended question.

Coding

The coding of the open-ended question was approached with the
goals of (1) developing a strategy that was simple enough to minimize
the number of categories and difficult, error-inducing coding decisions and (2) accurately and fully reflecting the range of responses
given by survey participants. Both the extant literature on the drug-
testing debate and a preliminary reading of the respondents' answers
suggested the main categories in which reasons for and against drug-
testing programs would fall. Overlapping and multiple responses
were allowed, so if a person supporting drug testing wrote, "It can
improve productivity and safety in the workplace," the response
would be coded for concerns with both productivity and safety. It
was generally quite obvious whether a comment was for or against
testing, and no more than 3 percent of the pro- or antitesting subgroups cited issues listed here as supporting the other position. The
coding categories and a description of the coding standards are as
follows.

Antitesting Responses

1. Privacy or Autonomy. Responses coded into this category include such things as the basic and common "violates right to
   privacy," or "it's not anybody's business what's in my urine,"
   or "my life is my business." The organizing principle for this
   category was the stressing of personal autonomy and or the
   privacy in which to exercise that autonomy.
2. Explicit Legal Arguments. For a response to be coded into this
   category, it had to make a specific reference to a right, the
   Constitution, the Bill of Rights, an amendment, or something
   like the slightly more general legal construct "innocent until
   proven guilty." Obviously, one would expect a good deal of
   overlap between categories measuring a privacy claim and a
   rights claim, since someone who responded, "violates my
   right to privacy," would be coded for both. (Of the 286 people
   coded into one of the two categories, 64 were in both.)

3. Test Error. Included here were any responses centering on the possibility of error on drug tests. "False positives," "tests not perfected," "poppy seeds and tea test as heroin," or "they make mistakes" are examples of statements marking concern over the accuracy of the technology.

4. Harassment or Discrimination. This category includes such comments as, "they would be used to single out troublemakers," "who's to say that management won't just test the people they don't like," or "they will be used to discriminate." A few people argue that the whole idea of drug testing was an effort to discriminate against labor in general, but these were excluded from this category because the focus is on the use of test administration to discriminate against individuals or, potentially, small groups within the workplace.

5. Unnecessary or Ineffective Policy. As the quotations indicate, responses in this category question whether testing programs are really needed or would be an effective policy to meet problems which may exist.

6. Dignity. These responses raised the concern over compelled and/or observed urination and raise challenges to the demeaning nature of urine testing.

7. Surveillance. Responses here addressed a perception of increasingly widespread surveillance and control. Here, testing was seen as "one more step" in a broader pattern.

8. Not Performance Related. Concerns had to do with the fact that drug tests measure neither current impairment nor job performance and thus are an illegitimate tool for employers to use.

9. Class Politics. The entries complained of the unfair portrait of workers implied by the drug testing initiative or framed the issue as a management campaign to harass and oppress workers in general.

Pro-testing Claims

1. Workplace Safety. The most often cited reasons for supporting testing were found in this category. Any response that centered on concerns over accidents, injury, death, safety, or

the danger that drug-influenced individuals create was included in this category.

2. The General Drug Problem. This category includes references
   to the national drug problem or the War on Drugs or general
   comments about the undesirability of drugs. The organizing
   principle is that the respondent provide a pro-testing reason
   that does not center on the workplace—"drugs are against the
   law," "we have to fight the national problem," and "drugs are
   wicked" are examples of responses in this category.

3. Productivity. This category includes concerns over the quality
   or quantity (mostly the former) of work produced by drug-
   using colleagues. "Drugs make workmanship less reliable,"
   "drug users aren't as good at what they do," and "we all have
   to pick up the slack from the drug user" are exemplary.

4. Elimination of Drug Users from Workplace. Statements coded
   made no specific reference to safety or productivity, but expressed a general antipathy to being around drug users, the
   belief that testing would ensure a better workforce, or a statement along the lines of "drugs do not belong in the
   workplace."

5. Treatment. Responses here center on getting medical help or
   counseling for substance abusers and the belief that drug testing could help to identify those people.

Appendix 2

The Focus on
Federal Decisions

Conflict over testing programs has been situated in a variety of institutional settings. A few state legislatures and municipalities have taken action to either support, limit, or simply regulate drug-testing programs (see Cornish 1988, 327–63). Hundreds of workplace contracts have been negotiated, ranging from the widely influential Master Freight Agreement of the Teamsters to countless minor contracts between union locals and individual employers. Numerous cases have gone to arbitration in conflicts between union members and employers (Coulson 1987; Denenburg and Denenburg 1987; Veglahn 1989). There have also been a limited number of tort claims by discharged employees or claims made under provisions in various state constitutions (see Cornish 1988, 210–51). But the center of attention for the press, the public, and decision makers in the arenas just mentioned are cases at the federal court level, especially those involving the Supreme Court.

The federal cases heard thus far have primarily addressed questions surrounding the constitutionality of drug-testing programs.[1] Of course, for a constitutional question to be raised, there must be an element of state action involved; the constitution only directly limits the action of the government, and cases from the private sector do not normally fit this profile. Therefore, the federal cases studied here have involved government employees or others affected by government policies who are challenging the government's right to use drug testing in the workplace.

While these cases may thus appear to be of limited importance in that they technically apply only to those workers employed by some level or extension of government, they are actually of much wider influence. The federal court decisions influence not just those people directly affected but, less directly, the millions of other workers encompassed by decisions made in the arenas mentioned above. First of all, the scope of the state action decisions does include a large number of those American workers who have faced testing programs. One in every six workers is employed by some level of government, and under the Fourteenth Amendment, cities, states, and counties are subject to the standards set for the federal government. Additionally, workers not employed by the government but who face testing programs under legislative or administrative policy will also normally have a constitutional claim because their employer is carrying out government policy (Bible 1987, 617–18).[2]

While the possibility of formal state action[3] or public policy[4] extensions of federal court decisions seems slim in the current legal climate, there is a less formalized tendency for standards developed in the federal courts to be applied in both tort law and private sector arbitration. One who reads those arbitration decisions that have been published[5] quickly notes that the language and standards the arbitrators use are almost exactly the same as those federal judges use (see also Hebert 1988, 859; Veglahn 1989). As Denenburg and Denenburg explain in reference to standards for labor arbitration,

> Influenced by the general political/legal culture, arbitrators often derive "workplace rights" by analogy to constitutional and statutory rights. They tend to enforce such rights as part of the due process to which an employee is entitled in the system of industrial justice. (1987, 410)[6]

Bible makes a similar point in discussing private sector tort cases and argues that public law decisions "may well be used as roadmaps by courts confronted with challenges to private sector testing programs" (1989, 676; see also Heshizer and Muczyk 1988, 352–53; Veglahn 1989). In *Luedtke v. Nabors Alaska Drilling, Inc.*, for instance, the judge "relied on federal court Fourth Amendment cases in resolving the claim that a private company's urinalysis program impermissibly invaded the plaintiff's state constitutional and common law privacy rights" (Bible 1989, 677 n.12). Similarly, in *Brotherhood of Locomotive Engineers v. Burlington Northern Railroad*, the Ninth Circuit held that postaccident testing by a private company violated Fourth Amendment rights to privacy that were seen as implicit in a collective bargaining agreement.

Finally, there is the somewhat amorphous cultural and political impact of federal court—especially Supreme Court—opinions in setting expectations in an area like this one. My interviews with union leaders clearly showed that the Supreme Court's decisions in *Skinner v. Railway Labor Executives' Association* and *National Treasury Employees Union v. Von Raab* were closely watched as a reference point for negotiation in both public and private sector industries. In contract negotiations or prenegotiation discussions with employers attempting to implement testing programs, such a central decision on the legitimacy of testing programs has an important role as bargainers search for some common ground on which to work. Further, as seen above, both employers and union representatives can expect common law and arbitration proceedings to be shaped by public sector decisions.

In a variety of ways, then, the public sector cases centering on the constitutionality of employee drug testing shape the national context and general policy standards surrounding employee drug testing. Yet one must be careful not to go too far in stressing the importance of the federal standards. Arbitrators may be more or less responsive to privacy claims than key federal opinions, and state constitutions and legislation may create more or less concrete claims to privacy. Further, of course, millions of employees in the nonunionized blue collar and service industries never make claims because they lack the organization, money, and leverage to do so. While bearing these caveats in mind, I believe that the public law decisions of the federal courts are the best place to begin an analysis of the overall response of "the law" to the employee drug testing controversy.[7]

Notes

Chapter 1

1. Hippocrates lived some twenty-four centuries ago and Galen roughly eighteen.

2. Overviews of the rise of testing include Ackerman 1991 and Zimmer and Jacobs 1992. Walsh and Trumble (1991) provide an unabashedly pro-testing account in Coombs and West 1991. Walsh is director of applied research at the National Institute on Drug Abuse and has been one of the most central players in the development and implementation of employee drug testing.

3. This describes the experience of an employee in the Georgia Power testing program designed by Peter Bensinger and discussed in chapter 3.

4. See *Seattle Times*, March 8, 1989 A1, U.S. Dept. of Labor 1989. These issues are discussed more thoroughly in chapter 3. As noted below, a positive test result does not show that someone is working under the influence of drugs. It only shows that they have been exposed to drugs at some point in the relatively recent past—up to two months in the case of marijuana. Critics of testing also note that illegal drug use is a far less significant problem than more widespread and costly alcohol use. Therefore, the massive expenditure and attention devoted to drug testing depletes resources from this and other problems and may fight a real interest in health and safety (McBay and Hudson 1987, 578–79).

5. We will see that the accuracy problem is also a very complex issue because it appears to be playing the role of a red herring in some key fights over testing. Accuracy concerns are not really an argument against testing or other forms of surveillance; rather, they are a request that testing be done well. Such an argument clearly falls short of criticizing the idea of surveillance itself. Further, in chapter 4, we will see that while nearly two-thirds of surveyed workers feel that drug tests are "likely to make mistakes," this concern is not as important as many other issues in the drug-testing debate. In this way, the focus on accuracy that was seen in court cases and arguments in the 1980s may actually work against and erode the more fundamental concerns over privacy and other problems with testing.

6. See Dubowski 1987; Maugh 1986; Morgan 1984; Willette 1991 for discussions of drug-testing techniques.

7. *Screen testing* refers to the use of an inexpensive and often inaccurate test to do a first sweep of a population. Those samples that test positive for drug use on the screen test are then subjected to verification through another test.

8. In that Gaventa specifically states that his concept of power includes the process of controlling whether or not people think it is even necessary to rebel, I think that Scott (1985, 325 n.43) is mistaken in implying that Gaventa rejects the idea of ideological hegemony.

9. The term *resistance* has been subject to extensive debate and analysis, and I rely here on Scott's broad definition. Thus, it is used interchangeably with the term *opposition* to refer to the primarily litigious antitesting actions taken by workers or their representatives. Obviously, worker sentiments and union law suits do not make up the full face of resistance and opposition—changing jobs, cheating on tests, negotiation battles, and other means of expression would have to be included. In an ongoing project studying welfare clients' responses to computerized number matching, the multifaceted concept of resistance is more central to a discussion of the use of barter, undeclared cash income, and black market activities to resist the state's total surveillance of recorded financial activity. Here, however, the focus is almost exclusively on the area of rights claims and litigation.

10. Beliefs such as this may be supported by the fact that many judicial decisions in the last fifty years have represented significant victories for claims to civil rights and liberties (Abraham 1988; Baum 1989, 187–88). Baum's analysis, however, shows that the success of civil liberties claims in Supreme Court decision making has dropped sharply since the 1970s (1989, 189).

Chapter 2

The William Bennett epigraph was taken from his speech at the Washington Hebrew Congregation, May 1989 (Morley 1989, 346).

1. Joseph Gusfield's seminal *Symbolic Crusade* (1963) pursued these issues in analyzing the social history of the temperance movement in late nineteenth- and early twentieth-century America. Gusfield argues that what we see in the moral reform efforts of the temperance movement—obviously comparable to the current War on Drugs—is "one way through which a cultural group acts to preserve, defend or enhance the dominance and prestige of its own style of living" (1963, 3). By drawing our attention to the conflict of groups contending for dominance and prestige, Gusfield reminds us that the process of identifying and dealing with social problems is, after all, an arena of political conflict. Efforts to define and respond to social problems, in short, must be evaluated from a perspective concerned with relations of power. Playing out this focus, Gusfield's final analysis portrays the focus on alcohol use and the temperance movement itself as the eventually unsuccessful response of a threatened rural Protestant middle class to the rising position of urban immigrant laborer groups (1963, chap. 6).

2. I will not be making this last and essentially functionalist argument in the case at hand. Arguing that events leading to social change were caused by the need for that change is problematic because it inverts the temporal ordering normally associated with causal arguments. I will argue, however, that the events studied here do contribute to the types of social change discussed by Hall et al. (1978).

3. These figures—like any data on societal drug use—should not be viewed uncritically. Along with the usual risks of survey data is the problem of basing the surveys in households or high schools and thus excluding those who are not part of such institutions. Further, there is the risk of relying on people to self-report illegal drug use, especially in a period of rising social and legal sanction. On the other hand, NIDA's field workers do make every effort to ensure confidentiality and never even see respondents' answers to questions, which are written on a form that contains no identifying information (NIDA 1990, 7).

4. An eleven-year overview of high school seniors based on studies conducted by NIDA shows that levels of use among young people declined since 1979 for marijuana and held largely steady since 1980 for cocaine (NIDA 1987, 46–51).

5. NIDA asks if the respondent has used a substance in the last thirty days, the last year, or ever in the respondent's lifetime. Obviously, the reporting rates go down as the time span narrows. The thirty-day measure is used here because that is how NIDA defines regular use, and it seems to be the only category that gets beyond measuring singular or occasional experimentation.

6. When we remind ourselves that the Reagan administration's War on Drugs preceded the emergence of crack by nearly two years, the relationship between problem and policy grows even more tenuous.

7. The project was supported and published by the Robert Woods Johnson Foundation.

8. Data from the 1988 report of the Drug Abuse Warning Network (DAWN) shows that among 4,678 drug deaths reported by urban emergency rooms, there is normally (72.1 percent) more than one drug found in the autopsy, and medical examiners list them in their reports. The first on the list is "alcohol-in-combination" (that does not include deaths due to alcohol alone), second was cocaine, then came heroin. The prevalences of these top three were nearly equivalent with mentions between 1572 and 1730. A combined category for marijuana and hashish was listed in the seventeenth position and was never seen as a principle cause of death (NIDA 1988, 58). This last point is an important one in that the vast majority of employment and police actions in relation to drug use have to do with marijuana (see Trebach 1987, 80–81). While deaths related to cocaine use in metropolitan areas have risen sharply since the early 1980s, the absolute figures are minuscule in a national sense: 983 deaths in 1987 were linked to cocaine in combination with drugs such as alcohol and heroin, and 207 deaths were attributed to cocaine alone. These figures exclude New York City, which, according to Kerr (1986),

had no cocaine-related deaths in 1982 and 137 in 1985. Zimring and Hawkins (1992) suggest that DAWN's 1987 figure may be inflated because of overreporting by doctors caught up in the drug crisis mentality.

9. Michael Lipsky and David Olson document one of the best examples of these phenomena in showing that while race riots in the mid-1960s received extensive and dramatic media coverage, by the late 1960s and early 1970s press coverage declined while riots persisted (1977, 446–47).

10. The coining of the new term for the processed version of cocaine bears important similarities to the use of the term *mugging* in Hall et al.'s *Policing the Crisis* (1978). The invention of the new term for common street larceny created an illusion of something entirely new, more threatening, and foreign in crime reporting during the London crisis. Similarly, the use of the term *crack* distinguishes it from the, by then, common drugs such as heroin and cocaine and has the symbolic impact of creating a sense of new and urgent crisis.

11. Indeed, when President Reagan announced Executive Order 12564, implementing drug testing for millions of federal workers, the ever-vigilant White House press corps grilled him with the following questions:

Q: Do you have a cold?

A: What?

Q: Do you have a cold? Are you suffering from a cold?

A: . . . It isn't a cold; no it's an allergy.

Q: How do you feel?

A: Other than that, I'm feeling fine.

Q: You're not taking any drugs for the—[inaudible]—antihistamines? [Laughter]

A: No, Sam [Donaldson, ABC]. I irrigate my nasal passages with salt water.

Q: Just say no.

See Public Papers of the President, Sept. 15, 1986, 1183; more broadly, see Hertsgaard 1988.

12. One of her favorite centers was Straight Inc., which is also endorsed by drug-testing advocate Robert DuPont. It has been the subject of numerous successful civil suits for wrongful imprisonment, the intentional infliction of emotional distress, and assault and battery (see Trebach 1987, 19–63).

13. Reagan's attitude toward drug use has been clear since at least 1969, when he and his California staff attested to a link between marijuana use, radicalism, and anarchy (*San Francisco Chronicle*, September 19, 1969, 7).

14. The President's Commission on Organized Crime challenged earlier supply-side approaches to controlling drug use—attempts to cut off the importation of illegal drugs were not doing the job. The commission thus recommended a demand-side approach to eliminating drug use and called for harsher sentencing of users and small dealers and for the widespread use of urine testing by both public and private sector employers (see 484–85).

15. In relation to the drug issue, it may be of some importance that marijuana use has a strong cultural association with leftism, hippies, 1960s per-

missiveness, and anti–Vietnam War politics. Perhaps the New Right's attack on drug use is partly explainable as an attack on a perceived lifestyle element of their political enemies (see Gusfield 1963; Kaplan 1970, chap. 1). Note the congressional testimony of drug-testing consultant Robert DuPont (OSHA Oversight Hearings 1985, 3): "You remember, in the sixties, there were concerns in the workplace about whether people could have mustaches or beards, for example. Companies eliminated codes of dress. There was a lot of concern about freedom of individual determination about behavior at work. Drug use got swept up in that kind of thinking."

16. It could also be argued that the "new behaviorists" simply ignore the causes of deviance to center on preventing the deviant behavior through the use of rewards and punishments (Cohen 1985, 147–54). Under either interpretation of their views, however, the resulting policies are likely to be dense surveillance and firm discipline.

17. In contrast, structuralist interpretations trace the origin of individual behavior to social conditions. They would focus official resources on improving those environmental conditions that are linked with chronic drug abuse and providing assistance for deviants (who are seen as victims of circumstance). They are likely to have greater tolerance for individual deviance given the lesser concern with incentives and disincentives in the microeconomy of social control. Hall et al. (1978) argue that the mugging crisis featured in their study was not best seen as a street crime crisis (i.e., caused by bad people) but as more broadly symptomatic of an economic and political crisis of state authority (i.e., part of a bad society). A similar tension is seen here. Volitional explanations of deviance center on individual failure and, often tacitly, assert an otherwise reasonable world. Structural explanations, on the other hand, force the issues of social and economic organization and therefore raise arguments similar to some of those brought up by Hall and his colleagues.

18. As noted in the opening lines of this book, the United States now has the highest rate of incarceration in the world; the Justice Department links the bulk of the increasing prison population to drug enforcement convictions (Seattle Times, May 21, 1990, A5). The social control initiatives affiliated with the War on Drugs have been markedly authoritarian and punitive (see Zimring and Hawkins 1992; Wisotsky 1986, 1987a). Federal expenditure on punitive drug law enforcement (such agencies as the Federal Bureau of Investigation [FBI], the DEA, and the Bureau of Prisons) skyrocketed during the War on Drugs. Budget allocations have risen from a 1981 outlay of $707.6 million to a 1985 outlay greater than $1.2 billion. By 1989, these criminal justice and interdiction efforts sections of the drug control budget were up to over $4 billion, while prevention and treatment were slightly over $1.5 billion. Throughout this period, federal expenditure on prevention, education, and treatment has been roughly a third of its punitive efforts; the formal and largely realized goal of 71 percent law enforcement and 29 percent treatment and education represents a real and significant punitive emphasis to drug control strategy (see Office of Drug Abuse Policy 1984, 121–23; Office

of National Drug Control Policy 1989, 1–12; Zimring and Hawkins 1992). For an overview of what Wisotsky calls the increase of "Big Brotherism" under the auspices of the War on Drugs, see chapter 7 of his *Breaking the Impasse in the War on Drugs* (1986).

Chapter 3

The Bensinger epigraph appeared in *U.S. News and World Report*, March 17, 1986, quoted in Guererro 1987, 23.

1. The workplace may also be a social setting in which legal limits on traditional law enforcement officers are inapplicable, thus offering less ground for resistance or opposition to various control bids. See chapter 5's discussion of administrative searches.

2. Social control policies such as these are the natural outcome of the conservative law and order philosophy discussed in the preceding chapter. As noted, proponents of this view see misbehavior as a rational choice that can be decisively affected through strategies of deterrence. Deterrence policy traditionally has three basic goals: the certainty of apprehension, the certainty of swift sanction, and the severity of sanctions. Our focus here is on the first element, certainty of apprehension.

The implementation of drug testing throughout the most pervasive institutions of our society creates a net of surveillance that, if fully implemented, could almost guarantee the certainty of apprehension. Surveillance policies like drug testing, computer number matching, and drunk driver checkpoints therefore emerge as a central and crucial part of the deterrence equation. We will return to these issues in reviewing court decisions on drug testing in chapter 5.

3. See, for example, *ABA Journal*, August 1, 1986, 35; *Atlanta Journal and Constitution*, November 16, 1986; *Los Angeles Times*, October 29, 1986.

4. The rail programs were uncommon in that they included tests for the presence of alcohol; most industrial programs test strictly for the use of illicit drugs or prescription drugs that are subject to abuse. The forty-three positive results include a few cases in which more than one substance was identified in a single individual.

5. Basing his evaluation on the forensic analysis of drivers in automobile accidents, North Carolina's chief toxicologist concluded, "There is no evidence that drugs other than alcohol are involved in a significant number of accidents" (McBay 1987, 647).

6. 53 Fed. Reg. 16641 (1988). The FRA was unclear on the source of those previous estimates. Despite this conclusion, the FRA that had rejected random testing as "unfair" in 1985 proposed it in 1988 (American Federation of Labor and Congress of Industrial Organizations [AFL-CIO], amicus brief, *Skinner v. Railway Labor Executives' Association*).

7. Perhaps suggesting that these are firms that tend to have a higher prevalence of drug use in their work force.

8. While the results were announced with a front-page headline in the *Seattle Times* declaring, "Drug-testing Snares 203 Federal Employees," when the reader followed the article back to page 5, it was learned that the 203 positives were out of a pool of 30,307 workers. The headline was alarming, but the test results were not—in percentage terms, the positive rate was 0.7 percent.

9. In several workplaces where drug testing was pursued due to executive order—most notably the Customs Department and the Department of Justice—administrators informed the executive that there was no significant drug problem. When the Labor Department then proposed that an evaluation of drug use in the federal workplace be made prior to massive federal expenditure on testing, President Reagan refused (Wisotsky 1987b, 766).

10. See also Ferguson and Rogers 1986, 134: "At OSHA . . . enforcement of existing law dropped precipitously, while the development of new workplace standards came to a virtual halt."

11. While OSHA—the subject of Noble's analysis—is obviously quite different than drug testing, there is a key parallel: in seeking safety, they both fail to empower the workers. In assessing OSHA's failure to live up to its promises, one key factor Noble identifies is that OSHA did not sufficiently enable workers to take care of themselves. He argues that it was largely a statist policy, in which the government was responsible for inspections and enforcement. Giving these responsibilities to an executive agency left the program especially vulnerable to political pressure and change, as we've seen in the 1980s.

12. By the early 1990s, however, EAP practitioners were apparently embracing testing as a means of identifying potential clients (Jacobs and Zimmer 1991, 348).

13. According to the translator's note to *Discipline and Punish*, the English word *discipline* was only chosen after much deliberation. Bentham had used the word *inspect*, Foucault, the French term *surveiller;* the intended meaning of the term is revealed in that the two close contenders for the first word of the title were *supervise* and *observe*. In my view, it is unfortunate that in the process of translation, a word that downplays the simple process of watching was chosen. (Foucault 1979, "Translator's Note").

14. This account is summarized and explained in his lecture of January 14, 1976. See Foucault 1980b.

15. See Foucault 1980b, 91; Dreyfus and Rabinow 1983, 130–31. The latter make the intriguing suggestion that many aspects of Foucault's discourses or systems of power can be thought of as akin to Kuhn's paradigms (see Dreyfus and Rabinow 1983, 197–200). They also offer one of the most cogent overviews of Foucault's views of the history of punishment and discipline (Dreyfus and Rabinow 1983, 144–60).

16. There is disagreement among some scholars over how one would identify truly disciplinary methods in relation to such endeavors as social work and crime control (see Cohen 1979, 1985; Nelken n.d.). But at a general level centering on the expansion of surveillance and the elimination of devi-

ance, there seems little room to doubt that a program akin to employee drug testing manifests what Foucault meant by the disciplines.

17. In that one of the most important features of urine testing is its ability to bypass the subjects' intellectual ability to lie, cheat, disagree, or explain, Foucault's work on the relation of mind and body as objects of discipline becomes especially important. At the same time that the techniques of surveillance and discipline emerge, Foucault identifies the emergence of a conceptualization of the body as an object and target of power (1979, 136–37).

18. It is worth noting that proponents of these forms of social control also see legal claims as a primary source of opposition to their programs. Amitai Etzioni and Richard Remp, who study and endorse a variety of monitoring and surveillance techniques in their *Technological Shortcuts to Social Change*, complain that "we seem to have difficulty creating a favorable legal context for the effective use of quantitative breath tests" (1973, 87). They go on to note that technological control methods are readily acceptable in the military but that there seems to be a rights-based social bias against them in other contexts (see Etzioni and Remp 1973, 87–88; see also chap. 5).

19. In one sense, these two accounts might seem to be fundamentally at odds. Foucault, on the one hand, treats disciplinary and juridical systems of control as antithetical discourses. Edwards, on the other hand, unites disciplinary and law-based means of control into one system called "bureaucratic control." But note that Foucault argued that, *in practice*, disciplinary and legal forms would undoubtedly appear and work together (see 1980b, 105–6). The two discourses, then, may have been theoretically distinct but could coexist in practical terms. Edwards, while treating these two modes as part of one approach to the practice of social control, notes that one can be played off the other and thus points to the tension that is more central to Foucault's analysis. While their emphases are pulled in different directions by the focuses on theory and practice, I think that there is far more similarity than difference.

20. Foucault makes a pretty safe bet. As explained in chapter 1, the language of rights so thoroughly permeates the political culture that it is almost surprising when people do not turn to their "famous formal right[s]."

Chapter 4

The Taylor epigraph is from his *The Principles of Scientific Management*, as quoted in Braverman 1974, 105.

1. Commitments made to the survey participants and the facilitating organization prevent the use of specific names or locations involved in this research. The vast majority of those in the profession are male; virtually all are high school graduates, and a majority have had some college.

2. Responses were entered on a scale of one (strongly support) to five (strongly oppose) with a "Don't Know" option to the right of the scale. Unless otherwise noted, textual references to supporters and opposers refer to those who feel either strongly or moderately this way. In the interest of

readability, percentages are rounded off to the nearest whole number in the text of this report. In explaining their views on random testing, several respondents felt that union activists or "troublemakers" would be "randomly" selected more often than others.

3. One might reasonably wonder why there is even this much opposition to a program that would only affect job applicants, but the situation in a craft area such as this one is unlike many other occupations. Jobs tend to be of shorter duration than other industries—especially in the construction field— and thus preemployment testing may, in effect, constitute a fairly regular application of tests to the working population. One interviewed craftsperson from another, though similar, field felt that although his union had successfully opposed random testing, it had "been suckered" because the high rate of job turnover in his field meant that the preemployment testing would actually imply a fairly dense schedule of tests.

4. It is worth noting that accident-triggered testing receives less support than suspicion-based testing and more middle-of-the-road responses than any other program. This type of program is of great interest to employers because in OSHA-required record keeping and in any potential liability disputes, there is an important difference between an accident caused by an impaired employee's error and one caused by an environmental or mechanical factor. Employers thus have a considerable interest in thoroughly investigating the possibility of employee impairment. While forensic scientists point out that a drug test is not capable of showing that drug use caused an accident (McBay and Hudson 1987; Morgan 1988), the tests are nonetheless used in ways that imply that they can.

5. Union leaders expressed great dismay upon learning of this distribution. Their response reflects the difficulty of the political situation this creates for them—no matter which course of action is taken, there will be a number of disgruntled members.

6. In discussing the composition of the main subgroups in the survey population, clarity and efficiency are served by selecting or creating one basic measure of the dependent variable showing whether an individual is basically for or against drug testing. This was done by using the measure of whether or not the respondent wants the union to oppose drug testing as both a theoretically important and empirically accurate gauge of views on drug testing. Theoretically, this project is most strongly concerned with the nature of political action surrounding drug-testing programs. For the population studied in this survey, the most obvious and likely course of mobilization over workplace issues is through its union. Whether a worker supports or opposes testing, the union is the body through which both conflict and action are most likely to go. Therefore, a respondent's opinion on whether or not that person wants the union to oppose or support drug-testing programs provides a very important measure of attitudes that are likely to translate into actual political action.

From an empirical perspective, as well, views on union policy provide a sound general measure of opinion on this topic. As seen above, there are somewhat differing relations among different programs; some who support suspicion-based testing, for instance, strongly oppose random testing, and this distinctive relationship must be addressed. But in general, there is a strong correlation between the union policy views and the respondents' views on specific programs. The correlations show that the variable measuring desired union policy and views on the four different programs are closely linked ($p < .001$). Given these empirical and theoretical assets of the single variable measuring desired union policy, the following analysis of the sub-

Correlation between Preferred Union Policy and Position on Specific Testing Programs

	Pre-employment	Random	Suspicion-based	Post-accident
Association with union policy (R)	.73	.62	.63	.57
N	754	749	749	744

groups will use the division over union policy as the primary dividing line. Of course, important points that have emerged involving difference between this and other measures of policy preference will be addressed as they arise.

7. Since many respondents gave more than one reason to support their views on testing, tallies add up to more than 100 percent.

The importance of uncued, open-ended questions is revealed in, for example, the sharp difference in the results for open- and close-ended questions about testing and treatment. On a scaled question asking whether the respondent agreed with the statement, "Drug testing helps users get treatment," fully 74 percent of the pro-testing group agreed that it did (indeed even 25 percent of the antitesting group agreed). Yet on the noncued question, not even 4 percent mentioned this as a reason for supporting testing. Thus, while the treatment issue may be agreed on when introduced by the survey, it does not seem to be high on the agenda of much of the membership.

8. In presenting these quotations, I have taken the liberty of correcting the spelling where necessary but have not edited for grammar except with a few bracketed additions to improve flow or to replace specific references to names or terms that would disclose the identity of those surveyed. For reference purposes, the individual case number is provided in the parentheses following each quotation.

9. As expected, there is a fair amount of overlap between this category and that expressing claims about privacy—of the 286 people in either category, 64 were in both.

10. There is an alternative approach to the data that is not disconfirmable on the basis of the research design used here. The point raised by, for example, Daryl Bem, would suggest that those who for some reason oppose drug testing will tend to discount the problem situation that drug testing is presumed to be a response to. Thus, rather than presuming that perception leads to preferred policy response, it may be argued that preferred policy response leads to perception. The only way to test such a proposition would be to establish some objective assessment of a situation and study variance in assessments among groups with different policy preferences. While this may be possible in highly controlled experiments, it is impossible in a real world setting in which individuals have different experiences and sequences of experiences, when the situations being assessed are only loosely bounded in time and space, and in which competition between priorities and definitions prohibit the establishment of an objective assessment of a situation.

11. Etas express the percentage of variance in the dependent variable that is explained by the independent variable.

12. Correlations are based on the full five-point scale.

13. This observation should be tempered with the caution that survey questions about privacy and rights were directly related to drug testing, while the assessment of the drug problem was asked in general terms (see appendix 1). Given this difference, there may have been a higher tendency for pro-testing and antitesting workers to check off positions on rights and privacy that support their view on testing. That could also be done on the drug problem assessment, but the question asked there did not specifically raise the topic of drug testing although the overall survey was clearly addressing that topic. The high correlation ($r = .75$ and $.79$, respectively) that the privacy variable and the rights variable have with desired union policy may suggest that these measures are to a considerable extent tapping the same phenomena.

14. It also suggests that the "myth of rights" (Scheingold 1974) plays an important role in public perception and evaluation.

15. While there may be some question whether general claims to privacy should be classified as legalistic claims, I believe that it is appropriate to do so. First, the workers themselves provide a strong indication of the linkage : fully 45 percent of those who make a privacy claim use explicitly legal language in making it. Second, there is the broader cultural tie evident in the fact that much contemporary law has dealt with the issue of privacy (Breckenridge 1970; Hixson 1987). Third is the fact that these claims become explicitly legal as they are advanced in almost any form of conflict over testing. Whether in contract negotiations, arbitration hearings, or, of course, outright court cases, the claim to privacy takes on the color of law. These three points are all quite different, but each points to the propriety of framing the privacy claims as legalistic.

16. That is not to argue that these workers necessarily hold a naive faith in the "myth of rights" (Scheingold 1974). It is more likely that their use of rights terms is based on more realistic beliefs about the limits of law (Merry

1986; Milner 1989). Different research techniques—probably relying on more ethnographic means of research—would be necessary to say whether these rights claims are advanced because of a deep belief in rights, because of political strategy, or because of a lack of alternatives.

17. Scott encountered a similar situation on the issue of land reform in the Malaysian village of Sedaka. While peasants never raised the issue themselves, they uniformly and enthusiastically supported this fundamental reformation of class relations when Scott raised it. Scott concludes that land reform was not a realistic approach to their problems and that the peasants were focused on more practical strategies of self-improvement in the existing system. He argues that cultural hegemony may be best understood as the ability to "define what is realistic and what is not realistic" (1985, 325–26).

Chapter 5

1. The pages that follow deal with many different issues, testing programs, and judges in an attempt to make sense of a judicial debate that sometimes appears to be senseless. Since there are so many different varieties of testing programs and an even greater variety of administrative details within programs, it would be unworkable to attempt a case-by-case analysis of each and every decision's findings in relation to the variety of possible circumstances and programs. Therefore, this analysis will center on the judicial response to antitesting claims seen in the preceding chapter as opposed to a case-by-case history.

2. The California Supreme Court, however, let stand a state court's decision against random drug testing on the basis of that state's constitutional right to privacy (*Luck v. Southern Pacific Transportation Co.*). In federal cases, the *Griswold* tradition sometimes arises in discussions of the privacy attached to medical information that is unrelated to drug use but required by some testing programs.

3. As Bookspan put it, "Although the word privacy does not appear in the fourth amendment, that meaning is found to be implicit" (1987, 310).

4. While there are important differences among these classes of testing programs, they all dispense with individual suspicion as the starting point for an inspection of the citizenry. As argued in chaper 3 and below, the emergent forms of social control represented by testing require an ongoing search or, at least, the ongoing threat of a search. The individual suspicion threshold must be overcome for these types of programs to work. This chapter thus devotes most of its attention to the courts' response to those testing programs and parts of programs that do not include some element of individual suspicion. That is the central issue in terms of both privacy protection and the analysis of social control policy.

5. "Probable cause" evades precise definition but is best thought of as something "more than bare suspicion" and "less than evidence which would justify . . . conviction" (*Brinegar v. United States*, 338 U.S. at 175; see Lewis 1990, 1013).

6. See appendix 2 for a discussion of why the focus here is on federal cases rather than other legal arenas.

7. There is wide agreement on the basic question of whether or not a urine test constitutes a search in the meaning of the Fourth Amendment. According to the widely influential standard first put forth in the Harlan concurrence to *Katz v. United States*, two standards must be met for a judge to decide that a search has occurred. "[F]irst that a person have exhibited an actual [subjective] expectation of privacy and, second, that the expectation is one that society is prepared to recognize as 'reasonable'" (389 U.S. at 361). To my knowledge, only one federal judge has argued that a drug test was not a search (*Lovvorn v. City of Chatanooga*, 6th Cir., Guy, J., dissenting). The wide agreement that a urine test is a search is based on the argument that the subjective and social criteria put forth in the *Katz* test are easily met in the case of compelled urination and the analysis of bodily fluids.

8. In making a distinction between the Fourth Amendment and due process, I make a somewhat artificial delineation because the two are so totally intertwined. The provisions of the Fourth were, for instance, extended largely under the cover of the due process provisions of the Fourteenth Amendment. Similarly, due process in the selection of those to be searched has often been expressed under Fourth Amendment law. At this point in history, due process refers to such a broad array of values that separating it out from other constitutional provisions is difficult, if not impossible. Nonetheless, there are a few key aspects of the drug-testing debates that are best addressed in separate terms.

9. Chief Justice Burger was a key advocate of this view (for discussion, see Abraham 1988, 131–51; Walker 1989, 246–52).

10. Juanita Jones was a Washington, D.C., school bus attendant discharged after all transportation employees were subject to EMIT-type tests in the summer of 1984. She sued, and the center of the decision was the school district's reliance on an unconfirmed EMIT test and its failure to provide any form of hearing mechanisms through which the accused could dispute the results of the test.

11. These standards were developed under pressure from Democratic members of Congress and in the context of several successful lawsuits challenging the accuracy of testing programs. On the accuracy dimension, as emphasized in the final chapter, lawsuits over testing have produced significant improvements for federally covered workers, though job applicants and other less protected populations still face major problems in this area.

12. Obviously, then, they were not random.

13. Although in *von Raab*, one aspect of the program, the testing of employees who handle "classified material," was suspended pending a clarification of what class of employees is actually included in this category.

14. The issues that might have been addressed by the Court include whether tests are a form of self-incrimination prohibited by the Fifth Amendment, whether the tests violate privacy interests recognized under a penumbra surrounding explicit constitutional rights, and whether job actions on the

basis of such tests violate due process standards. But while these issues have
been important elements in some lower court decisions, in workers' arguments, and in academic debates over drug testing, the Court limits itself to a
discussion of whether the tests meet the reasonableness standards of the
Fourth Amendment on questions of their inception, scope, and lack of individualized suspicion. For a comprehensive overview of potential issues, see
Bookspan 1987; Fogel, Kornblut, and Porter 1988.

15. The lengthy advance notice and the lack of direct observation render
this program toothless as a serious tool for identifying many drug users. All
but heavy marijuana users or addicts should be able to have their own urine
clean prior to the test, and those that are unable to do so can carry clean urine
into the stall in a water bottle strapped to the body. The proximity to the
body maintains temperature, and a small tube creates the judicially approved
"sounds of normal urination."

16. Because of the extensive overlap between these two cases, the discussion that follows addresses the key issues of each by focusing on *Skinner*.
Where important differences arise, they are indicated.

17. However, James (1988) does feel that if a particular workplace can be
shown to have a serious drug use problem, then it may be reasonable to
search all employees.

18. In addition to the Fourth Amendment issues, the Court discussed the
due process issues of accuracy and fairness. Each issue was handled with
some dispatch. The question of accuracy was dealt with in a footnote: "Respondents have provided us with no reason for doubting the FRA's conclusion that the tests at issue here are accurate in the overwhelming majority of
cases" (*Skinner*, 489 U.S. at 633 n.10). Kennedy rejected fairness concerns by
arguing that the search was so mechanical and highly regulated that the
possibility of abused discretion was minimal (489 U.S. at 622 n.6).

19. See chapter 3 for a review of other problems surrounding the efficacy
of testing and the alleged lack of alternatives.

20. One problem with applying the administrative search exception in
these cases is revealed by looking at the Ninth Circuit's opinion in the railroad testing case. After reviewing the history of the administrative search
exception, the court here concluded,

> We do not believe the administrative inspection exception is applicable to
> the regulatory scheme before us. All of the decisions in this line of cases
> have upheld warrantless searches of property, not of persons, and we
> decline to make such an extension in this case. . . . There is no question
> that the railroad industry has experienced a long history of close regula-
> tion. This regulation has diminished the *owners'* and *managers'* expecta-
> tions of privacy in railroad premises, but we do not believe it has dimin-
> ished the individual railroad *employee's* expectation of privacy in his person
> or body fluids. (*Burnley*, 839 F.2d at 585, citation omitted)

21. In portraying the *Skinner* tests as noncriminal, Kennedy argues that
there is no indication that the searches are *intended* to serve as a guise for
criminal searches. But when faced with the question whether the use of

evidence from administrative searches in criminal proceedings would taint the definition of an administrative search, his response was to move the question to a footnote and save it for "another day" (489 U.S. at 621 n.5). Worth noting here is the comment of the district court in *Allen v. City of Marietta*: searches of potential wrongdoing by government employees "always carry the potential to become criminal investigations" (601 F. Supp. at 491). As ruled in one of the earliest drug-testing cases: "If the inspections are legal, any evidence of crime obtained therefrom may be used in criminal action" (*Committee for GI Rights v. Callaway*, 518 F.2d at 475).

22. After complaining that "about the only clear thing about balancing are the techniques for putting the judicial thumb on the scale" (Shapiro 1966, 85), Shapiro notes that the court will often play fast and loose in defining the opposing sides of a balancing act. In his critique of the use of balancing in free speech cases, he wrote, "Ad hoc balancing has proven so satisfactory to anti-libertarians precisely because they could portray each individual infringement on speech not as a subordination of the general principle of freedom of speech to some other principle, but as a tiny, little, temporary interruption of the speech of a few people to avoid a tremendous blow to the interests of mother, country, and apple pie" (Shapiro 1966, 91).

23. But Justice Stevens's concurrence offers good reason for doubt: "I think it a dubious proposition that the regulations significantly deter the use of alcohol and drugs by hours of service employees. Most people . . . do not go to work with the expectation that they may be involved in a major accident. . . . Moreover, even if they are conscious of the possibilities that such an accident might occur and that alcohol or drug use might be a contributing factor, if the risk of serious personal injury does not deter their use of these substances, it seems highly unlikely that the additional threat of loss of employment would have any effect on their behavior" (489 U.S. at 634).

24. Scalia dissented in this case because he saw no evidence of a drug problem in the Customs Agency.

25. The Customs program has no visual monitoring.

26. Although the main focus of both this essay and broader attention to the Supreme Court opinion has been tied to the now widely used urinalysis method of drug testing, some parts of the program in *Skinner v. Railway Labor Executives' Association* also include blood tests. The FRA's program is unique in using these far more costly tests along with urinalysis; even the FRA only gathers blood for the most extreme category of accidents. In discussing the blood tests' intrusiveness, Kennedy notes that while blood tests are a search and are invasive of the body, they are not troublesome because they are "performed in a reasonable manner, as the . . . blood [is] taken by a physician in a hospital environment according to acceptable medical practices" (489 U.S. at 625, citing *Schmerber v. California*). He goes on to argue that we have grown so familiar with the blood tests associated with the standard medical examination that 'the blood test procedure has become routine in our everyday life'" (489 U.S. at 625, quoting *Breithaupt v. Abram*). The ability of blood tests to more precisely measure actual levels of the drugs or alcohol in the

system means that some of the legal arguments made against the less accurate urine tests might not apply. In that some of the resistance to urinalysis
has been based on the argument that this method cannot reveal current
impairment (see James 1988), it may be that cheaper and more generally
accessible means of blood analysis will mitigate these concerns. At this point
in time, however, even blood tests cannot successfully show how impaired
the employee is. Until the link between blood concentration and impairment
is reliably understood, blood tests remain open to scientific challenge as a
measure of actual impairment (Cornish 1988, 16–18).

27. A number of authors have turned their attention to the role of medical
language, technology, and personnel in implementing systems of social control (see, for instance, Donzelot 1979; Illich 1976; Roman 1980). Medicalized
language and policies have been seen as particularly invulnerable to challenge by those who have been defined as "patients" (Edelman 1977; Roman
1980). That the involvement of medical personnel in these programs works
to significantly mitigate oppositional claims to privacy values does not bode
well for future legal resistance to what Roman calls "the medicalization of
control" (1980).

28. Kennedy shows that these types of tests are effectively random for the
railroad employee who cannot "predict with certainty" when accidents occur;
accidents occur with some regularity in industry, and to use them to trigger
testing is to set up a largely randomized testing policy.

Chapter 6

1. "Following *Von Raab*, courts may find that every government employee whose position may be made potentially dangerous by the use of
drugs can be subjected to drug testing without any evidence of drug use by
the individual or his or her peers" (Dean 1990, 406).

2. Random testing of Department of Transportation employees was approved for motor vehicle operators and hazardous materials inspectors
(*American Federation of Government Employees v. Skinner*); Boston police officers
who carry guns or work in drug interdiction are subject to random testing
(*Guiney v. Roaches*); annual surprise testing for sheriff's deputies who work
with prisoners was allowed (*Taylor v. O'Grady*); random testing for armed
security personnel, vehicle drivers, and those with top secret clearance was
allowed, but not random testing of data processors (*American Federation of
Government Employees v. Cavasos*); random testing of civilian army employees
in aviation and law enforcement was upheld, but not random testing of EAP
workers (*National Federation of Federal Employees v. Cheney*).

"Federal Courts have generally upheld the various testing programs"
(Lewis 1990, 1038), but there have been several cases in which judges have
knocked down a program or parts of it on the grounds that *Skinner* and *von
Raab* did not control. *American Federation of Government Employees v. Thorn-
burgh: von Raab* does not apply to random testing of all Federal Bureau of
Prison employees, and the agency failed to target job functions with "special

needs"; *Hartness v. Bush*: random testing of all federal employees in the General Services Administration (GSA) and Executive Office of the President was enjoined because there was no evidence of a drug problem or threat; *Harmon v. Thornburg*: *von Raab* does not apply to random testing of all Justice Department employees involved in criminal prosecutions but does apply to those with top secret security clearance or drug enforcement responsibilities.

3. National opinion surveys taken prior to the 1980s' mobilization of the War on Drugs revealed far greater support for values of privacy and autonomy than more recent surveys (compare Harris 1979 and ABC News 1988).

4. Ideological hegemony is not equivalent to the problematic idea of "false consciousness," as some authors imply (Cohen and Rogers 1983, 51). The idea of false consciousness is an epistemological anachronism because it rests on the outmoded idea of a singularly true reality that is autonomous of ideology and belief (Hunt 1985; McCann 1989, 238).

> If a consciousness exists, it is real to its holders, and thus to the power situation. To discount it as "false" may be to discount too simply the complexities or realities of the situation. *What is far more accurate (and useful) is to describe the content, source, or nature of the consciousness—whether it reflects awareness of certain interests and not of others, whether it is critical or assuming, whether it has been developed through undue influence of (power holders), and so on.* (Gaventa 1980, 29, emphasis added)

The goal, therefore, is to explore how, from multiple possible emphases and interpretations, these workers appear to have chosen the ones that they did. In this process of selection, if they have privileged an interpretation of events and a course of action that sacrifices important interests and advances the goals of those who would control them, then this might be seen as a manifestation of ideological hegemony (see Gaventa 1980, 15–16).

5. Such programs are far cheaper than drug tests and provide immediate feedback on the employee's ability to work. The ACLU appears to support these programs, arguing that they are accurate and do not constitute an invasion of privacy (see *Civil Liberties*, No. 370, Summer 1990, 7).

6. A fine-tuned understanding of ideological hegemony at the individual level would require a program of research different from that pursued here. In-depth ethnographic interviews as well as personal biographical information would be required to be more specific about how and if these processes work at the individual level.

7. Compare *Shoemaker v. Handel* with *Capua v. City of Plainfield*.

8. The expansive view of rights put forth by the Warren Court covered a wide variety of liberal changes in the law: *Miranda* rights, the right to counsel, civil rights, limits on internal security, and the right to privacy, to name only the most prominent (Baum 1989, 187–88; Schmidhauser 1984, 429–95). It was in this period that the Fourth Amendment limits on the state's power to search were most clearly and broadly developed. It is here, I think, that the contemporary legal interpretation of the Fourth Amendment that could limit suspicionless workplace drug testing would be found.

In taking these positions on criminal due process, privacy, and other rights, the Supreme Court "became extremely prominent and central in the nation's life" (Wasby 1984, 10). The political conflict over the Court and its decisions was expressed in Richard Nixon's 1968 campaign promise to rein in liberal judges who were hindering law enforcement with a "barbed wire of legalism" and turning criminals loose to victimize the silent majority (Schmidhauser 1984, 498). Once elected, he moved to appoint justices—including current Chief Justice Rehnquist—who were less bound to the due process movement, and the Court became "more conservative on civil liberties" (Wasby 1984, 11). Under the Reagan administration, with Rehnquist's elevation to chief justice and the appointment of three young conservative justices, the turn against the Warren Court rulings was dramatically strengthened. As Goldman explained,"Ronald Reagan with the help of Attorney General Edwin Meese III is responsible for a major change in the makeup of the Federal judiciary that will likely be a major legacy of the Reagan presidency. The most important change has the potential to fundamentally alter the civil liberties and civil rights Americans enjoy under the federal Constitution. . . . The Administration has declared war on judicial activism which it sees as having brought about . . . the rights of criminal defendants including the exclusionary rule and the Miranda warnings, and the right to privacy" (Goldman 1989, 307).

9. There are many other realms of action and possibilities to express opposition. In both state and federal courts, there remains a good deal of debate to this day—indeed, the California Supreme Court outlawed most forms of random testing in the late spring of 1990. The case, *Luck v. Southern Pacific Transportation Corp.*, turned on the fact that California's constitution has an explicit right to privacy, something its federal counterpart lacks. The fact that arbitrators had shown a tendency to support opposition to testing more strongly than the Supreme Court may mean that workers covered by collective bargaining agreements can take action in this venue. On the other hand, students of arbitration have seen an informal pattern in which arbitrators sometimes follow the path of the courts: "If the scales of the federal judiciary continue to shift so as to place more weight on societal concerns and less on individual rights and liberties, then arbitrators in the private sector are likely to follow suit" (Kirk 1989, 538). It should also be noted that by the late 1980s, seven states had enacted legislation regulating testing: Connecticut, Iowa, Minnesota, Montana, Rhode Island, Utah, and Vermont (U.S. Department of Labor 1989). All except Utah serve to restrict employers' freedom to test.

Appendix 2

1. However, some important cases, including one at the Supreme Court level, have addressed whether private sector testing constitutes a major or minor contract change under labor law. In *Consolidated Rail Corp. v. Railway Labor Executives' Association*, the Supreme Court classified conflict over a new

requirement of generalized drug testing during regular medical examinations as a minor one given a history of regular medical examinations. As a minor dispute under the Railway Labor Act, the dispute was subject to binding arbitration, rather than new bargaining. See Plass 1990, 61–73.

2. *Skinner v. Railway Labor Executives' Association*—a case involving private sector railroad workers tested under government policy—falls into this category and is addressed at length in Chapter 5.

3. One circuit court gave broad meaning to the state action argument by suggesting that constitutional provisions could apply to arguably private acts in light of the government's role in emphasizing the concern over illegal drugs and leading the antidrug campaign (*Railway Labor Executives' Association v. Burnley*). The court cited *United States v. Guest* in arguing that even if the government was just one force or player involved in a potential constitutional violation, then Fourth Amendment standards could be brought to bear. Given the federal government's promotion of employee drug-testing programs in all workplaces, it could be concluded under this logic that state action is involved in almost any drug-testing program (see *Burnley* 839 F.2d). It seems unlikely, however, that the Rehnquist Court would pursue such an expansive state action policy in light of its professed judicial conservatism and support for the autonomy of the private sector.

4. Public sector decisions may potentially affect private sector policy through public policy exceptions to the autonomy of private employers. As Hogler (1987–88) explains, if constitutional limits were placed on drug-testing programs, then judges could decide that private employers could not take action that subverts the public policy against testing. The best example of this is *Novosel v. Nationwide Insurance Co.*, which held that a private employer could not enforce a policy that violated an employee's right to free speech and association. If a legitimate expectation of privacy were to emerge that was comparable to free speech protections, then such public policy exceptions could create limits for the private sector. "That is, an 'unreasonable' search under the Fourth Amendment might also, as a matter of public policy, violate a private-sector employee's privacy rights" (Hogler, 1987–88, 490).

5. Decisions are only published if both parties agree, and in the controversial area of drug use and personnel policy, many participants have been unwilling to make their cases public.

6. See also Kirk 1989, 538: "If the scales of the federal judiciary continue to shift so as to place more weight on societal concerns and less weight on individual rights and liberties then arbitrators in the private sector are likely to follow suit."

7. Naturally, the best approach would be to study all the manifestations and applications of the law—common-law cases, arbitration, contracts, company policies, etc.—but such a task is beyond the means of the current project. On another point, both the oddity and the importance of the distinction between public and private sector employees should be noted. A feeling that one's privacy is being invaded is unlikely to distinguish between whether it is the government or a corporation that is doing the invading.

Such a violation is felt by the individual and is not necessarily linked to who or what is doing the violating. Yet our liberal legal tradition makes a fundamental distinction between the public and private realm. Thus, although rights claims can directly challenge the action of the state, they may not directly apply to corporations, which, although they may be more powerful than many states and nation-states, are treated as private persons. Therefore, the law may fail to express the legal claims of millions of workers and job applicants at the most fundamental level: the courts may refuse to say that important elements of the law can even be used by this wide class of grievants. As argued above, the legal standards that emerge from the federal cases are likely to have an impact in these other workplaces, but it is important to recognize that it is only an indirect one.

Bibliography

ABC News. *Drug Abuse Poll, 1986* (ICPSR 8636). Ann Arbor, Mich.: ICPSR, 1988. (The data used were originally collected by ABC News in a random sample of 2,326 American adults. Neither the collector of the data nor the consortium bear any responsibility for the analysis or interpretations presented here.)

Abraham, Henry J. *Freedom and the Courts: Civil Rights and Liberties in the United States.* New York: Oxford University Press, 1988.

Ackerman, Deborah L. "A History of Drug Testing." In *Drug Testing: Issues and Options,* Robert H. Coombs and Louis Jolyon West, eds. New York: Oxford University Press, 1991.

Adamany, David. "Legitimacy, Realigning Elections, and the Supreme Court." *Wisconsin Law Review* 73 (1973): 790–846.

American Federation of Labor and Congress of Industrial Organizations (AFL-CIO). *Drugs and Alcohol on the Job: Safety with Personal Dignity.* Washington, D.C.: AFL-CIO, 1987.

American Medical Association, Council on Scientific Affairs. "Scientific Issues in Drug Testing." *Journal of the American Medical Association* 257, no. 22 (June 12, 1987): 3110–14.

Aron, Martin. "Drug Testing: The Employer's Dilemma." *Labor Law Journal,* March 1987, 157–65.

Axel, Helen. "Drug Testing in Private Industry." In *Drug Testing: Issues and Options,* Robert H. Coombs and Louis Jolyon West, eds. New York: Oxford University Press, 1991.

Bachrach, Peter, and Morton S. Baratz. "The Two Faces of Power." *American Political Science Review* 56 (1963): 947–52.

Baer, Judith. "The Fruitless Search for Original Intent." In *Judging the Constitution,* Michael McCann and Gerald Houseman, eds. Boston: Scott Foresman, 1989.

Baum, Lawrence. *The Supreme Court.* Washington, D.C.: Congressional Quarterly Press, 1989.

Bennett, Lance. *Public Opinion in American Politics.* New York: Harcourt, Brace, Jovanovich, 1980.

———. *News: The Politics of Illusion.* New York: Longman, 1988.

Bentham, Jeremy. "Panopticon, or the Inspection-House, etc." In *The Works of Jeremy Bentham*, vol. 4, John Bowring, ed. New York: Russell and Russell, 1962.

Bible, Jon. "Employee Urine Testing and the Fourth Amendment." *Labor Law Journal*, October 1987, 611–40.

———. "Update: Employee Urine Testing and the Fourth Amendment." *Labor Law Journal*, November 1989, 675–91.

Bookspan, Phyllis T. "Behind Open Doors: Constitutional Implications of Government Employee Drug Testing." *Nova Law Review* 11 (1987): 307–70.

———. "Jar Wars: Employee Drug Testing, the Constitution, and the American Drug Problem." *American Criminal Law Review* 26 (1988): 359–400.

Bork, Robert. *Tradition and Morality in Constitutional Law*. Washington, D.C.: American Enterprise Institute, 1984.

Braverman, Harry. *Labor and Monopoly Capital: The Degradation of Work in the Twentieth Century*. New York: Monthly Review Press, 1974.

Breckenridge, Adam. *The Right to Privacy*. Lincoln: University of Nebraska Press, 1970.

Brigham, John. *Civil Liberties and American Democracy*. Washington, D.C.: Congressional Quarterly Press, 1984.

Bumiller, Kristen. "Victims in the Shadow of the Law: A Critique of the Model of Legal Protection." *Signs* 12 (1987): 421–39.

Burawoy, Michael. *Manufacturing Consent: Changes in the Labor Process Under Monopoly Capitalism*. Chicago: University of Chicago Press, 1979.

Bureau of National Affairs. "Drug Testing and EAPs." In *Employee Assistance Programs: Benefits, Problems and Prospects*. Washington, D.C.: BNA Special Reports, 1987.

Carter, Lief, and John Gilliom. "From Foundation to Discourse: Trends in Contemporary Constitutional Philosophy." In *Judging the Constitution*, Michael McCann and Gerald Houseman, eds. Boston: Scott Foresman, 1989.

Cobb, Roger, and Charles D. Elder. *Participation in American Politics: The Dynamics of Agenda-Building*. Baltimore: Johns Hopkins University Press, 1975.

Cohen, Joshua, and Joel Rogers. *On Democracy: Toward a Transformation of American Society*. New York: Penguin, 1983.

Cohen, Stanley. "The Punitive City: Notes on the Dispersion of Social Control." *Contemporary Crises* 3 (1979): 339–63.

———. *Folk Devils and Moral Panics*. New York: St. Martins, 1980.

———. *Visions of Social Control*. Cambridge: Polity Press, 1985.

Coombs, Robert H., and Louis Jolyon West, eds. *Drug Testing: Issues and Options*. New York: Oxford University Press, 1991.

Copelon, Rhonda. "Beyond the Liberal Idea of Privacy: Toward a Right of Autonomy." In *Judging the Constitution*, Michael McCann and Gerald Houseman, eds. Boston: Scott Foresman, 1989.

Cornish, Craig M. *Drugs and Alcohol in the Workplace*. Willamette, Ill.: Callaghan and Co., 1988.

Coulson, Robert. *Alcohol, Drugs, and Arbitration*. New York: American Arbitration Association, 1987.

Crenshaw, Kimberle. "Race, Reform, and Retrenchment: Transformation and Legitimation in Antidiscrimination Law." *Harvard Law Review* 101, no. 7 (May 1988): 1331–87.

Crenson, Matthew A. *The Unpolitics of Air Pollution.* Baltimore: Johns Hopkins University Press, 1971.

Curran, William J. "Compulsory Drug Testing: The Legal Barriers." *New England Journal of Medicine,* February 5, 1987, 318–21.

Dahl, Robert. "Decision-making in a Democracy: The Supreme Court as a National Policy Maker." *Journal of Public Law* 6 (1957): 279–95.

Dean, Harlin Ray. "The Fourth Amendment Hangs in the Balance." *North Carolina Law Review* 68 (January 1990): 389–409.

Denenburg, Tia Schneider, and Richard V. Denenburg. "Drug Testing from the Arbitrator's Perspective." *Nova Law Review* 11 (1987): 371–413.

Donzelot, Jacques. *The Policing of Families.* New York: Pantheon, 1979.

Douglas, Mary, and Aaron Wildavsky. *Risk and Culture.* Berkeley: University of California Press, 1982.

Dreyfus, Hubert, and Paul Rabinow. *Michel Foucault: Beyond Structuralism and Hermeneutics.* Chicago: University of Chicago Press, 1983.

Dubowski, Kurt M. "Drug-Use Testing: Scientific Perspectives." *Nova Law Review* 11 (1987): 415–552.

Edelman, Murray. *The Symbolic Uses of Politics.* Urbana: University of Illinois Press, 1967.

———. *Political Language: Words That Succeed and Policies That Fail.* New York: Academic Press, 1977.

———. *Constructing the Political Spectacle.* Chicago: University of Chicago Press, 1988.

Edwards, Richard. *Contested Terrain.* New York: Basic Books, 1979.

Ehrlich, Isaac, and R. Mark. "Fear of Deterrence: A Critical Evaluation of the 'Report of the Panel on Research on Deterrent and Incapacitative Effects.'" *Journal of Legal Studies* 6 (1977): 293–316.

Ellul, Jacques. *The Technological Society.* New York: Vintage, 1964.

Etzioni, Amitai, and Richard Remp. *Technological Shortcuts to Social Change.* New York: Russell Sage Foundation, 1973.

Ferguson, Thomas, and Joel Rogers. *Right Turn: The Decline of the Democrats and the Future of American Politics.* New York: Hill and Wang, 1986.

Flannery, Harry. "Unilaterally Instituted Drug Screen Tests in the Unionized Private Industry: An Appropriate Response?" *Labor Law Journal,* December 1987, 756–62.

Fogel, Stephen M., Gerri L. Kornblut, and Newton T. Porter. "Survey of the Law on Employee Drug Testing." *University of Miami Law Review* 43 (1988): 553–697.

Foucault, Michel. *Discipline and Punish.* New York: Vintage, 1979.

———. *The History of Sexuality.* New York: Vintage, 1980a.

———. *Power/Knowledge.* Colin Gordon, ed. New York: Pantheon, 1980b.

Freeman, Alan. "Antidiscrimination Law: A Critical Review." In *The Politics of Law: A Progressive Critique,* David Kairys, ed. New York: Pantheon, 1982.

Funston, Richard. "The Supreme Court and Critical Elections." *American Political Science Review* 69 (1975): 795–811.

Galanter, Marc. "Why the 'Haves' Come Out Ahead: Speculations on the Limits of Legal Change." *Law and Society Review* 9 (1974): 95–160.

Gaventa, John. *Power and Powerlessness: Quiescence and Rebellion in an Appalachian Valley.* Urbana: University of Illinois Press, 1980.

Geertz, Clifford. *The Interpretation of Cultures.* New York: Basic Books, 1973.

Genovese, Eugene. *Roll, Jordon, Roll: The World the Slaves Made.* New York: Vintage, 1972.

Gitlin, Todd. *The Whole World Is Watching.* Berkeley: University of California Press, 1980.

Gladwell, Malcolm. "Drugs: The Abrupt Rise (and Demise) of the Latest Media Hype." *Insight,* October 27, 1986, 8–12.

Goldfield, Michael. *The Decline of Organized Labor in the United States.* Chicago: University of Chicago Press, 1987.

Goldman, Sheldon. "Reorganizing the Judiciary." *Judicature* 68 (1985): 313–29. Revised and reprinted in *American Court Systems: Readings in Judicial Process and Behavior,* Sheldon Goldman and Austin Sarat, eds. New York: Longman, 1989.

———. *Constitutional Law.* New York: Harper and Row, 1987.

———. "Reagan's Judicial Legacy." *Judicature* 72, no. 6 (April-May, 1989): 318–30.

Goldman, Sheldon, and Austin Sarat, eds. *American Court Systems: Readings in Judicial Process and Behavior.* New York: Longman, 1989.

Government Accounting Office. *Employee Drug Testing: Information on Private Sector Programs.* GAO/GGD-88.32. Washington, D.C.: Government Printing Office, 1988.

Gramsci, Antonio. *Selections from the Prison Notebooks.* Quinton Hoare and Geoffrey Smith, eds. New York: International Publishers, 1985.

Greenberg, Eric Rolfe. "Workplace Testing: The 1990 AMA Survey: Part 2." *Personnel,* July 1990, 26–29.

Greer, Edward. "Antonio Gramsci and Legal Hegemony." In *The Politics of Law: A Progressive Critique,* David Kairys, ed. New York: Pantheon, 1982.

Gross, Hyman. *Privacy—Its Legal Protection.* Dobbs Ferry, N.Y.: Oceana, 1976.

Guerrero, Gene. "The Federal Role: Uncle Sam or Big Brother?" In *Drug Testing: Protection for Society or a Violation of Civil Rights?,* minutes of the conference of the National Association of State Personnel Executives, Lexington, Ky., 1987.

Gusfield, Joseph. *Symbolic Crusade.* Chicago: University of Chicago Press, 1963.

———. *The Culture of Public Problems.* Chicago: University of Chicago Press, 1981.

Hall, Stuart. "Culture, the Media and the 'Ideological Effect.'" In *Mass Communication and Society,* James Curran, Michael Gurevitch, and Janet Woolacott, eds. Beverly Hills, Calif.: Sage, 1979.

Hall, Stuart, Chas Crichter, Tony Jefferson, John Clarke, and Brian Roberts. *Policing the Crisis: Mugging, the State, and Law and Order.* New York: Holmes and Meier, 1978.

Haltom, William. "Separating Powers: Dialectical Sense and Positive Nonsense." In *Judging the Constitution,* Michael McCann and Gerald Houseman, eds. Boston: Scott Foresman, 1989.

Hansen, Hugh, Samuel Caudill, and Joe Boone. "Crisis in Drug Testing: Results of a CDC Blind Study." *Journal of the American Medical Association* 253 (April 26, 1985): 2382–87.

Hanson, F. Allan. "Some Social Implications of Drug Testing." *Kansas Law Review* 36 (1988): 899–917.

Harris, Louis. *The Dimensions of Privacy: A National Opinion Research Survey of Attitudes toward Privacy.* Stevens Point, Wis.: Sentry Insurance, 1979.

Harstein, Harry. "Drug Testing in the Workplace: A Primer for Employers." *Employee Relations Law Journal* 12 (Spring 1987): 577–608.

Hebert, L. Camille. "Private Sector Drug Testing: Employer Rights, Risks, and Responsibilities." *Kansas Law Review* 36 (1988): 823–67.

Helmer, John. *Drugs and Minority Oppression.* New York: Seabury, 1975.

Hertsgaard, Mark. *On Bended Knee: The Press and the Reagan Presidency.* New York: Farrar, Strauss & Giroux, 1988.

Heshizer, Brian, and Jan Muczyk. "Drug Testing at the Workplace: Balancing Individual, Organizational and Societal Rights." *Labor Law Journal,* June 1988, 342–57.

Hixson, Richard F. *Privacy in a Public Society.* New York: Oxford University Press, 1987.

Hoffman, Abbie. *Steal This Urine Test.* New York: Penguin, 1987.

Hogler, Raymond. "Contractual and Tort Limitations on Employee Discipline for Substance Abuse." *Employee Relations Law Journal* 13 (Winter 1987–88): 480–500.

Hudner, Karen. "Urine Testing for Drugs." *Nova Law Review* 11 (1987): 553–61.

Hunt, Alan. "The Ideology of Law: Advances and Problems in Recent Applications of the Concept of Ideology to the Analysis of Law." *Law and Society Review* 19 (1985): 11–37.

Illich, Ivan. *Medical Nemesis.* New York: Random House, 1976.

Imwinkelried, Edward J. "Some Preliminary Thoughts on the Wisdom of Governmental Prohibition or Regulation of Employee Urinalysis Testing." *Nova Law Review* 11 (1987): 563–603.

Jacobs, James B. *Drunk Driving: An American Dilemma.* Chicago: University of Chicago Press, 1988.

Jacobs, James B., and Lynn Zimmer. "Drug Treatment and Workplace Testing: Politics, Symbolism and Organizational Dilemmas." *Behavioral Sciences and the Law* 9 (1991): 345–60.

James, Jeannette C. "Comment: The Constitutionality of Federal Employee Drug Testing: *National Treasury Employees Union v. von Raab.*" *American University Law Review* 38 (1988): 109–40.

Joseph, Paul R. "Fourth Amendment Implications of Public Sector Work Place Drug Testing." *Nova Law Review* 11 (1987): 605–45.

Kairys, David, ed. *The Politics of Law: A Progressive Critique*. New York: Pantheon, 1982.

Kamisar, Yale. "Drugs, AIDS, and the Threat to Privacy." *New York Times Magazine*, September 12, 1987, 109–14.

Kaplan, Elaine, and Lois Williams. "Will Employees' Rights Be the First Casualty of the War on Drugs?" *Kansas Law Review* 36 (1988): 755–85.

Kaplan, John. *Marijuana: The New Prohibition*. New York World Publishing, 1970.

Kennedy, Duncan. "Critical Labor Law Theory: A Comment." In "Forum on Labor Law." *Industrial Relations Law Journal* 4 (1981): 449–506.

Kerr, Peter. "Anatomy of an Issue: Drugs, the Evidence, the Reaction." *New York Times*, November 17, 1986, 1, 12.

Kirk, Geoffrey T. "Employee Drug Testing: Federal Courts Are Redefining Individual Rights of Privacy, Will Labor Arbitrators Follow Suit?" 44 *University of Miami Law Review*, November 1989, 489–538.

Krieger, Joel. *Reagan, Thatcher, and the Politics of Decline*. New York: Oxford University Press, 1986.

Lapham, Lewis. "A Political Opiate." *Harper's Magazine*, December 1989, 43–48.

Le Roy, Michael H. "Drug Testing in the Public Sector: Union Member Attitudes." *Journal of Collective Negotiations* 19, no. 3 (1990): 165–73.

Lewis, Andrea. "Drug Testing: Can Privacy Interests Be Protected under the 'Special Needs' Doctrine?" *Brooklyn Law Review* 56 (1990): 1013–44.

Lipsky, Michael, and David J. Olson. *Commission Politics: The Processing of Racial Crisis in America*. New Brunswick, N.J.: Transaction Books, 1977.

Lockhart, William B., Yale Kamisar, and Jesse H. Choper. *Constitutional Rights and Liberties*. 5th ed. St. Paul: West, 1981.

Lukes, Stephen. *Power: A Radical View*. London: MacMillan, 1974.

Lustig, R. Jeffrey. *Corporate Liberalism: The Origins of Modern American Political Theory, 1890–1920*. Berkeley: University of California Press, 1982.

McBay, Arthur. "Efficient Drug Testing: Addressing the Basic Issues." *Nova Law Review* 11 (1987): 647–52.

McBay, Arthur, and Karen Hudson. "Cost-Effective Drug Testing." *Journal of Forensic Sciences* 32 (1987): 575–79.

McCann, Michael. *Taking Reform Seriously*. Ithaca, N.Y.: Cornell, 1986.

———. "Equal Protection for Social Inequality: Race and Class in Constitutional Ideology." In *Judging the Constitution*, Michael McCann and Gerald Houseman, eds. Boston: Scott Foresman, 1989.

———. *Rights at Work: Pay Equity Reform and the Politics of Legal Mobilization*. Chicago: University of Chicago Press, 1994.

Maltby, Lewis. "Why Drug Testing Is a Bad Idea." *Inc.*, June 1987, 152–53.

Marx, Gary. "The Iron Fist in the Velvet Glove: Totalitarian Potentials within Democratic Structures." In *The Social Fabric: Dimensions and Issues*, James Short, ed. Beverly Hills, Calif.: Sage, 1986.

Marx, Gary, and Nancy Reichman. "Routinizing the Discovery of Secrets." *American Behavioral Scientist* 27, no. 4, (March/April 1984): 423–52.

Massing, Michael. "Two William Bennetts." *New York Review of Books*, March 1, 1990, 29–33.

Maugh, Thomas. "Drug Tests' Reliability Is Limited, Experts Say." *Los Angeles Times*, October 27, 1986.

Merry, Sally. "Everyday Understandings of Law in Working Class America." *American Ethnologist* 13 (1986): 253–70.

Miller, David A. "Mandatory Urinalysis and the Privacy Rights of Subject Employees: Toward a General Rule of Legality under the Fourth Amendment." *University of Pittsburgh Law Review* 48 (1986): 201–45.

Mills, John. *On Liberty*. New York: Bobbs Merrill, 1956.

Milner, Neal. "The Denigration of Rights and the Persistence of Rights Talk: A Cultural Portrait." *Law and Social Inquiry* 14 (1989): 631–75.

Morgan, John P. "Problems of Mass Urine Screening for Misused Drugs." *Journal of Psychoactive Drugs* 16 (October 1984): 305–17.

———. "Declaration in Support of Preliminary Injunction." *Berry v. District of Columbia*, No. 85-6158 (D.C. Cir. 1987).

———. "The 'Scientific' Justification for Urine Drug Testing." *Kansas Law Review* 36 (1988): 683–97.

Morley, Jefferson. "The Great American High: Contradictions of Cocaine Capitalism." *Nation*, October 2, 1989, 341–47.

Mulloy, Paul. "Winning the War on Drugs in the Military." In *Drug Testing: Issues and Options*, Robert H. Coombs and Louis Jolyon West, eds. New York: Oxford University Press, 1991.

Musto, David F. *The American Disease*. New Haven: Yale University Press, 1973.

National Association of State Personnel Executives and the Council of State Governments. *Drug Testing: Protection for Privacy or a Violation of Civil Rights?* Lexington, Ky.: Council of State Governments, 1987.

National Institute on Drug Abuse (NIDA). *Urine Testing for Drugs of Abuse.* Research Monograph #73. Rockville, Md.: National Institute on Drug Abuse, 1986.

———. *National Trends in Drug Use and Related Factors among American High School Students and Young Adults, 1976–1986*. Rockville, Md.: National Institute on Drug Abuse, 1987.

———. *Drug Abuse Warning Network: Annual Report 1987*. Rockville, Md.: National Institute on Drug Abuse, 1988.

———. *National Household Survey on Drug Abuse: Highlights 1990*. Rockville, Md.: National Institute on Drug Abuse, 1990.

Nelkin, David. "Discipline and Punish: Some Notes on the Margin." Manuscript.

Noble, Charles. *Liberalism at Work: The Rise and Fall of OSHA*. Philadelphia: Temple University Press, 1986.

Office of Drug Abuse Policy. *1984 National Strategy for Prevention of Drug Abuse and Drug Trafficking.* Washington, D.C.: Government Printing Office, 1984.

Office of National Drug Control Policy. *National Drug Control Strategy.* Washington, D.C.: Government Printing Office, 1989.

OSHA Oversight Hearings on the Impact of Alcohol and Drug Abuse on Worker Health and Safety Before the Subcomm. on Health and Safety of the House, 99th Cong., 1st Sess. (1985).

Packer, Herbert L. *The Limits of the Criminal Sanction.* Stanford: Stanford University Press, 1968.

Plass, Stephen. "A Comprehensive Assessment of Employment Drug Testing: Legal Battles over Delicate Interests." *San Diego Law Review* 27 (1990): 31–79.

Poster, Mark. *Foucault, Marxism and History.* London: Polity Press, 1984.

Preer, Robert M. "The Impact of Drug Testing." *Labor Law Journal,* January 1989, 50–57.

President's Commission on Organized Crime. *America's Habit: Drug Abuse, Drug Trafficking, and Organized Crime.* Washington, D.C.: U.S. Government Printing Office, 1986.

Pritchett, C. Herman. *Constitutional Civil Liberties.* Englewood Cliffs, N.J.: Prentice-Hall, 1984.

Reichman, Nancy. "Computer Matching: Toward Computerized Systems of Regulation." *Law and Policy,* October 1987, 387–415.

Rohan, Thomas. "Pushers on the Payroll." *Industry Week,* February 8, 1982, 53–57.

Roman, Paul. "Medicalization and Social Control in the Workplace: Prospects for the 1980s." *Journal of Applied Behavioral Science* 16, no. 3 (1980): 407–22.

Rosenberg, Gerald N. *The Hollow Hope: Can Courts Bring about Social Change?* Chicago: University of Chicago Press, 1991.

Rule, James B. *Private Lives and Public Surveillance.* London: Allen Lane, 1973.

Rule, James B., Douglas McCadam, Linda Stearns, and David Uglow. *The Politics of Privacy.* New York: Elsevier, 1980.

Sand, Robert. "Drugs in the Workplace: The Supreme Court, Congress, and the Federal Agencies Declare War." *Employee Relations Law Journal* 15 (Summer 1989): 125–34.

Schattschneider, E. E. *The Semi-Sovereign People.* New York: Holt, Rinehart, Winston, 1960.

Scheingold, Stuart. *The Politics of Rights: Lawyers, Public Policy, and Political Change.* New Haven: Yale University Press, 1974.

———. *The Politics of Law and Order.* New York: Longman, 1984.

———. "Constitutional Rights and Social Change." In *Judging the Constitution,* Michael McCann and Gerald Houseman, eds. Boston: Scott Foresman, 1989.

Schmidhauser, John. *Constitutional Law in American Politics.* Monterey, Calif.: Brooks/Cole, 1984.

Schneider, Elizabeth M. "The Dialectic of Rights and Politics: Perspectives from the Women's Movement." *New York University Law Review* 61 (1986): 589–652.

Schroeder, Elinor P. "On Beyond Drug Testing: Employer Monitoring and the Quest for the Perfect Worker." *Kansas Law Review* 36 (1988): 869–98.

Schulhofer, Stephen J. "On the Fourth Amendment Rights of the Law-Abiding Public." *1989 Supreme Court Review* (1989): 87–163.

Scott, James C. *Weapons of the Weak: Everyday Forms of Peasant Resistance.* New Haven: Yale University Press, 1985.

Shapiro, Martin. *Freedom of Speech: The Supreme Court and Judicial Review.* Englewood Cliffs, N.J.: Prentice-Hall, 1966.

Sigal, Leon V. *Reporters and Officials: The Organization and Politics of News Reporting.* Lexington, Mass.: Heath, 1973.

Silverstein, Helena, and Robert Van Dyk. "Social Movements in the Courts: Power and the Problems of a Legal Strategy." Paper delivered to the annual meeting of the Law and Society Association, June 1989.

Simpson, Duncan. "Does a 'Drug Free Federal Workplace' Also Mean a 'Fourth Amendment Free Workplace'?" *Labor Law Journal,* September 1989, 547–66.

Susser, Peter. "Legal Issues Raised by Drugs in the Workplace." *Labor Law Journal,* January 1985, 42–54.

Thompson, E. P. *Whigs and Hunters: The Origins of the Black Act.* New York: Pantheon, 1975.

Tocqueville, Alexis de. *Democracy in America.* J. P. Mayer, ed. New York: Anchor, 1969.

Trachtenberg, Alan. *The Incorporation of America: Culture and Society in the Gilded Age.* New York: Hill and Wang, 1982.

Trebach, Arnold S. *The Great Drug War.* New York: Macmillan, 1987.

Tushnet, Mark. "An Essay on Rights." *Texas Law Review* 62 (1984): 1363–1403.

U.S. Congress, House. 100/1, *Railroad Safety.* Y4. En 2/3 100–103.

U.S. Congress, House. *Dealing with Drugs and Alcohol in the Rail and Airline Industries.* Y 4.6 78/7 D84/22.

U.S. Department of Health and Human Services (DHHS). *Alcohol and Health* (1987).

———. *Reducing the Health Consequences of Smoking: A Report of the Surgeon General* (1989).

U.S. Department of Labor, Bureau of Labor Statistics. *Survey of Employer Anti-Drug Programs.* Washington, D.C.: Government Printing Office, 1989.

———. *What Works: Workplaces without Drugs.* Washington, D.C.: Government Printing Office, n.d.

Veglahn, Peter. "What Is a Reasonable Drug Testing Program? Insight from Arbitration Decisions." *Labor Law Journal,* October 1989, 688–95.

Walker, Samuel. *Sense and Nonsense about Crime.* Pacific Grove, Calif.: Brooks/Cole, 1989.

Walsh, J. Michael, and Jeanne G. Trumble. "The Politics of Drug Testing."

In *Drug Testing: Issues and Options*, Robert H. Coombs and Louis Jolyon West, eds. New York: Oxford University Press, 1991.

Warren, Samuel D., and Louis D. Brandeis. "The Right to Privacy." *Harvard Law Review* 4 (1890): 193–220.

Wasby, Stephen. *The Supreme Court in the American Judicial System.* Chicago: Nelson Hall, 1984.

Wasserstrom, Silas. "The Incredible Shrinking Fourth Amendment." *American Criminal Law Review* 21 (1984): 257–401.

Weisman, Adam. "I Was a Drug-Hype Junkie." *New Republic*, October 6, 1986, 14–17.

Weiss, Philip. "Watch Out: Urine Trouble." *Harper's*, June 1986, 56–57.

Westin, Alan F. *Privacy and Freedom.* New York: Atheneum, 1967.

Whitman, David. "The Streets Are Filled with Coke." *U.S. News and World Report*, March 5, 1990, 24–26.

Wildavsky, Aaron. "Richer Is Safer." *Public Interest* 60 (Summer 1980): 23–39.

Willette, Robert E. "Techniques of Reliable Drug Testing." In *Drug Testing: Issues and Options*, Robert H. Coombs and Louis Jolyon West, eds. New York: Oxford University Press, 1991.

Williams, Gurney, III. "Hair-Raising Science." *Omni Medical*, January–February 1990, 12–43.

Williams, Raymond. *Marxism and Literature.* New York: Oxford University Press, 1977.

Wilson, James Q. *Thinking about Crime.* New York: Basic Books, 1975.

Wisman, Eric W. "Peer Pressure Curbs Drug Use." *Personnel Journal* 69 (November 1990): 29–30.

Wisotsky, Steven. *Breaking the Impasse in the War on Drugs.* New York: Greenwood Press, 1986.

———. "Crackdown: The Emerging Drug Exception to the Bill of Rights." *Hastings Law Journal* 38 (1987a): 889–926.

———. "The Ideology of Drug Testing." *Nova Law Review* 11 (1987b): 763–78.

Zeese, Kevin B. "Drug Testing Here to Stay?" *George Mason University Law Review* 12, no. 4 (1990): 545–59.

Zimmer, Lynn, and James B. Jacobs. "The Business of Drug Testing: Technological Innovation and Social Control." *Contemporary Drug Problems*, Spring 1992, 1–26.

Zimring, Franklin E., and Gordon Hawkins. *The Search for Rational Drug Control.* New York: Cambridge University Press, 1992.

Zwerling, Craig, James Ryan, and Endel John Orav. "The Efficacy of Preemployment Drug Screening for Marijuana and Cocaine in Predicting Employment Outcome." *Journal of the American Medical Association* 264, no. 20 (November 28, 1990): 2639–43.

Index of Cases

Index

177